Financial Management for Student Affairs Administrators

John H. Schuh
EDITOR

American College Personnel Association
Media Publication No. 48

ACPA is a division of the
American Association for Counseling and Development

Distributed by University Press of America,® Inc.
4720 Boston Way, Lanham, Maryland 20706

Cover Design by Sarah Jane Valdez

Library of Congress Cataloging-in-Publication Data

Financial management for student affairs administrators.
(American College Personnel Association media publication:
no. 48)
1. Personnel service in higher education—United States—
Finance.   2. Student activities—United States—Finance.
3. Education, Higher—United States—Finance.   I. Schuh,
John H.   II. Series.
LB2343.F46   1990   378'.02'0973   89–18054

ISBN 1–55620–068–4 (pbk. : alk. paper)

 The paper used in this publication meets the minimum requirements of
American National Standard for Information Sciences—Permanence
of Paper for Printed Library Materials, ANSI Z39.48–1984.

The American College Personnel Association is a division of the American Association for Counseling and Development dedicated to serving students through professional programs for educators committed to student development. The Association unites the functions, services and programs of college and university student affairs professionals which include areas such as admissions, financial aid, counseling, career services, commuter programs, residence life, activities and health services. As the largest national professional organization of student affairs professionals with over 7,000 members, ACPA conducts ongoing professional development activities for members, provides the vehicle for profession-related social and political action, encourages human development and determines and maintains ethical standards in the profession.

The American College Personnel Association does not discriminate on the basis of race, color, national origin, religion, sex, age, affectional preference, or disability in any of its policies, procedures or practices. This non-discrimination policy covers membership and access to, association programs and activities including but not limited to National Conventions, placement, services, publications, educational services and employment.

Contents

About the Authors

John H. Schuh is Associate Vice President for Student Affairs at Wichita State University, Wichita, Kansas. He is editor and chair of ACPA Media and a past member of the Executive Board of ACUHO-I.

Margaret J. Barr is Vice Chancellor for Student Affairs at Texas Christian University, Fort Worth, Texas.

Linda M. Clement is Director of Admissions, University of Maryland-College Park, College Park, Maryland.

James A. Hyatt is Assistant Vice President for Resource Planning and Budgets, University of Maryland-College Park, College Park, Maryland.

George D. Kuh is Professor, School of Education, Indiana University, Bloomington, Indiana.

Donald B. Mills is Assistant Vice Chancellor of Student Affairs, Texas Christian University, Fort Worth, Texas.

Donald W. Nance is Director of the University Counseling Service, Wichita State University, Wichita, Kansas.

Michael S. Noetzel is Executive Assistant to the Chancellor of the Massachusetts Board of Regents of Higher Education, Boston, Massachusetts.

Elizabeth M. Nuss is Executive Director, National Association of Student Personnel Administrators, Washington, D.C.

Susan L. Pugh is Director of the Office of Student Financial Assistance, Indiana University, Bloomington, Indiana.

Jerry R. Quick is Associate Vice Chancellor for Business Affairs, Vanderbilt University, Nashville, Tennessee. He teaches a course on auxiliary services management at the University of Kentucky College of Business Management Institute.

Scott T. Rickard is Associate Dean, College of Liberal Arts, University of Maryland-Baltimore County, Catonsville, Maryland. He is past editor and chair of ACPA Media.

Debra Benoit Sivertson is Director of the Student Health Service, University of Maryland-Baltimore County, Catonsville, Maryland.

Introduction

"You know what really makes your rocket ships go up?"
"Hell, the aerodynamics alone would take so long to explain to you ..."
"Funding. That's what makes your ships go up. I'll tell you something. And you guys, too. No bucks—no Buck Rogers."

—Discussion in Pancho's Bar from the movie, *The Right Stuff*

On most campuses the same can be said for student affairs staffing and programming. Without adequate financial support, it is extraordinarily difficult to develop programs and services that address the out-of-class experiences of students. Room and board fees provide the revenue to support residence hall programs; sales of food and other commodities assist the student union program; fee money provides support for leadership development; and virtually every activity in student affairs requires some sort of financial support, be it in the form of direct funding, staff time, or office resources. In short, without appropriate funding, student affairs programs and services would not exist.

Perhaps naively, at times we in student affairs forget that only a few decades ago many of our services and programs did not exist in their present form. We did not have a counseling center or a financial aid office. Student housing was very limited, and even the office of the dean of students was just coming into being. So, student affairs history is not lengthy, and as the book's chapters will point out, student affairs administrators do not have a widespread reputation on many campuses as shrewd fiscal managers. Resources for our various programs have shrunk during the past decade, and there have been no systematic efforts to try to provide ideas and information about financial management for student affairs officers. Because of these and other issues, we decided it would be appropriate to develop a publication to address selected topics related to financial management for student affairs officers.

This book has several purposes. For the general reader, we hope it offers a perspective on the current financial environment. This environment is in marked contrast to the halcyon days of several decades ago when the national economy was more robust and funding for higher education was flush.

The chapter authors present a detailed view of several crucial, albeit expensive, services. A comparative approach has been taken to providing financial information about those services, and we believe that the external measures that have been used will make for useful comparisons.

We expect that this book will help young staff members understand and appreciate the linkage between financial support and student affairs services and programs. Frequently, in graduate preparation programs at the master's level, information concerning the financing of student affairs is addressed in a limited way. We believe that reading this book will enable the young professional to gain a better perspective on the critical role financial support plays in the development of student affairs programs and services.

We hope that this book will sharpen the sensitivity of staff in isolated departments to the issues colleagues in other student affairs departments face. For example, the director of a counseling center may not be cognizant of the issues involved in the financing of auxiliary services. Or, directors of financial aid and student health services may benefit from knowing more about budget issues in each other's area of specialization. We believe that this book will help people from disparate departments understand that there is not a single department in student affairs that does not face budget challenges.

This book has one other purpose. We hope that it will help student affairs officers improve their skills in fiscal and budgetary management. We hope that the ideas, concepts, and tips in this book will be of value to all student affairs officers, ranging from the veteran chief student affairs officer to the entering professional. Obviously, the seasoned budget manager will not find everything in this book new or remarkable, but we hope that no matter what their level of experience in student affairs resource management is, readers will find some useful ideas.

This book consists of nine chapters. The topics presented in these chapters, in our opinion, are some of the most important in the array of those that this type of publication might cover. After careful consideration, we decided not to include materials on such topics as accounting, fund-raising, special issues related to recreational sports programs, day-care centers and preschools, international student programs, and the like. Two reasons underscored our thinking along these lines.

One, we tried to select program areas prevalent in many student affairs divisions. Although we did not do an exhaustive survey to determine programs most common to student affairs, we believe that such areas as counseling, student health, admissions, and financial aids have captured and held the attention of student affairs administrators in our present financial environment. We thought that a chapter on accounting might lead to more detail than we wanted for this kind of publication, and a separate chapter on fund-raising, although useful to some student affairs administrators, would not have broad appeal. It is possible that this topic should be covered in the future as more student affairs divisions look to fund-raising from private sources to augment funds.

Two, we had to face several practical problems, and we wanted the authors to develop their topics as fully as possible given our space limitations, rather than introduce additional topics that would limit the length of the existing chapters.

A brief introduction of the nine chapters follows. In chapter 1 John Schuh describes the fiscal environment in which student affairs operates, and includes short discussions of various budgeting approaches. Don Mills and Peggy Barr, in chapter 2, point out some differences and similarities regarding fiscal management issues in independent and public institutions. Many of these differences are the result of the legal organization and control of a particular institution.

Trends in management information systems is the topic Jerry Quick addresses in chapter 3. He examines such issues as appropriate hardware and software, networking, training, and getting started. Linda Clement presents two aspects of financial management in the admissions office in chapter 4. She discusses the impact of enrollment on institutional revenues, and the management of the admissions office.

Susan Pugh, in chapter 5, identifies a series of questions appropriate to the management of the financial aids office. She discusses such matters as the unique issues related to financial aids, contemporary issues in the financial aids arena, and the tools available to financial aids officers. Don Nance provides a context for understanding the financial environment of counseling centers in chapter 6. He discusses current issues related to funding counseling centers and identifies sources of funding.

In chapter 7, Scott Rickard and Debra Sivertson identify current trends in student health services and describe seven funding models. The diverse models include centers funded entirely from allocated funds, from student health fees, combination-funded centers, fee-for-service centers, and contract and self-help models. Their discussion provides student affairs administrators with guidelines for comparing and contrasting the various student health service funding models.

In chapter 8, Mike Noetzel and Jim Hyatt describe major issues facing auxiliary services on college campuses and then present trends in the management of auxiliary services. For a variety of reasons, auxiliary services are increasingly being seen as sources of revenues for campus programs, but simultaneously they are being viewed with suspicion by private businesses and governmental taxing agencies.

In chapter 9, which concludes the book, George Kuh and Liz Nuss examine issues related to evaluating financial management in student affairs. They introduce the not-for-profit model as an interesting framework for evaluating student affairs.

I want to express my sincere appreciation for the patience and hard work of the chapter authors. They have been a delight to work with, xii

and they have made excellent contributions, in my judgment, to this effort. I also want to thank the members of the ACPA Media Board for their assistance in developing this project. They have been insightful in helping us sharpen our ideas and thoughts. And, I am very grateful to my colleagues at Wichita State University and Indiana University for their help with the technical aspects of this project. I thank Pat Davis and Cheryl Wolff for their marvelous help.

John H. Schuh
The Wichita State University
July 1989

CHAPTER 1

Current Fiscal and Budgetary Perspectives

John H. Schuh

This is not a pleasant time to be responsible for financing institutions of higher education. Costs of attending institutions are rising faster than inflation, support for state-assisted institutions is static or eroding, and questions are being raised as to the efficacy of expenditures for student affairs functions when resources might be better utilized in other parts of the institution. During the 1950s and 1960s, the growth of college and university resources was such that the era has been described as a golden age (McCorkle & Archibald, 1982), but as we move toward the end of this century, resources are much less plentiful. Farmer (1979) pointed out, for example, that concern about inflation, government costs, and demographic changes has plagued the financial health of higher education.

The purpose of this chapter is to describe the fiscal and budgetary environment in which we work. The first part of the chapter is devoted to introduce briefly some of the issues related to our financial environment. Then, strategies for student affairs are introduced, although these may not work on individual campuses. Finally, budgeting concepts are introduced. This section is not intended to be an exhaustive discussion of the various kinds of budgets one might encounter on various campuses, but it does define various budgetary approaches and points out some of their strengths and weaknesses.

THE FINANCIAL ENVIRONMENT

The Carnegie report *Three Thousand Futures*, released in 1980, identified a number of concerns about the foundations of higher education. Among these were that enrollment would fall considerably, that tax limitation movements would reduce fiscal resources available to higher education, and that public confidence in higher education would erode. The vision of the future that the commission ultimately adopted was more hopeful. It was an optimistic future in regard to the severe problems that confront higher education, with "reasonable solutions to most, if not all, of them" (Carnegie Council, 1980, p. 8). Indeed, Frances (1982) added that after the decade of the 1970s the quality of academic programs did not decline, for the most part, which was a great tribute to administrators and faculty (p. 113).

Since the publication of the Carnegie Council report, the fiscal resources available to many institutions of higher education have changed dramatically. In some cases more resources in constant dollars are available, whereas in others the picture of available resources is static or declining. A summary of state support of higher education (Mooney, 1987) indicated that a dozen states cut their budgets during the 1987 fiscal year, and that university officials in four more states listed financial survival as their top priority.

Students have not escaped higher education's fiscal dilemma. A report released in 1986 indicated that for 6 consecutive years college costs to students grew at a faster pace than the inflation rate (Evangelauf, 1986). Costs were predicted to outrun inflation for the balance of the decade. One of the results of these increasing costs is that one third to one half of all students leave college in debt. One estimate indicated that students leave private colleges with $8,950 in loans and public colleges with $6,685 in loans, on average (Evangelauf, 1987). Concerns have been expressed that a generation of students will leave college in debt as loans replace grants in financial aid awards (Hansen, 1984). Moreover, there is some evidence that parents are unwilling to pay what need-analysis services indicated they should (Hansen).

The response of the higher education community to students' problems has been modest. Attempts at solutions include tuition futures plans, tuition stabilization plans, and loan programs (Evangelauf, 1986). These approaches are variations on the long-standing history of student aid. They may have a negative side in that they can limit college choice and may be subject to changing federal, state, and local tax laws.

Nonetheless, higher education seems to be worth the cost. Bowen (1977) concluded that the resources expended are returned many times over. He wrote, "In short, the cumulative evidence leaves no doubt that American higher education is well worth what it costs" (p. 448).

One way that higher education might respond to the problem of inadequate resources is to become more efficient. Increasing efficiency, warned Bowen (1977), however, is full of pitfalls. He pointed out that simply cutting costs is not efficient if the outcomes sacrificed are considered more valuable than the product of the saved resources in another use. For example, if an ordinary program is replaced by a program that seems to be trendy but is poor in terms of its value to students, the result is worse than continuing the status quo. As new programs replace existing programs, we had better be sure that the net result will be an improvement in our overall portfolio.

Regardless on what improvements in efficiency are made, administrators in higher education seem committed to acquiring additional resources. Astin (1985) pointed out that one of the ways excellence is perceived in higher education is the accumulation of resources by institutions of higher education. He did remind us, however, that "resource-based conceptions of excellence tend to focus institutional energies on the sheer accumulation of acquisition of resources rather than the effective *use* of these resources to further the educational development of the student and to promote faculty development" (pp. 54–55). Thus, maybe the issue we should consider is not how to acquire more resources but how to use our present resources more wisely.

STUDENT AFFAIRS STRATEGIES

The prevailing financial environment creates difficult and challenging circumstances for student affairs administrators. Institutions of higher education, taken as an aggregate, have increasingly limited resources available to them, and internecine warfare among components of the academy tends to occur when genuine fiscal contraction begins to take place. Student services programs often have been viewed as easy targets during budget reductions (Pembroke, 1985, pp. 86–87). How might student affairs officers respond to this situation? Several suggestions follow.

Contribute to Institutional Programs

How do the student affairs division and its programs contribute to the programs of the institution? Pembroke (1985) pointed out that basic linkages between student affairs and academic programs have not been made at many institutions around the country. If the basic thrust of the institutions is undergraduate instruction, for example, what is being done in student activities, residential life, or the counseling center to promote undergraduate education? How do the activities of these departments complement the activities of the degree-granting units on campus? As Kauffman (1984) pointed out, ". . . all student services must relate to the specific mission and programs of an institution" (p. 27).

One approach to dealing with this issue would be for the chief student affairs officer, key staff, faculty, and students to review the mission statements of the various departments and programs in the division. Where the statements are vague, or less than direct in tying the department or program to the institution's mission, changes can be made through whatever process is appropriate for the division. Ultimately, the resulting statements ought to reflect the various ways that the student affairs division—its departments and programs—support and complement the institution's general programs and activities.

Measure Student Growth

After the programs of the student affairs division have been linked to those of the institution, another major issue to be resolved is how well the division is doing its job. Do student affairs programs and activities make a difference? If so, in what way? Do students grow as a result of student affairs programs? How are the academic progrms of the institution enhanced by those of student affairs? Kuh (1979) pointed out that "systematic *evaluation* of programs and personnel is necessary to insure that students are provided satisfactory services" (pp. 2–3). His thesis can be taken a step further in that not only should students be provided satisfactory services, but growth should be the result of student participation in student affairs programs and activities. Brown (1987) also called for continuing research efforts on programs that enhance the quality of student life and promote student development. In addition, he suggested that research might be done on how student affairs might enlist the support and allegiance of students, parents, faculty, and administrators for its efforts.

Measuring student growth is not always easy because so many variables intervene during the student's experience. It can be difficult to establish a causal relationship between student participation and growth. Nonetheless, Lenning (1980) made some helpful suggestions in the areas of assessment and evaluation. These include different types of evaluation, ways of linking evaluation with decision making, and staff skills and competencies needed for conducting assessments and evaluations. These recommendations provide a useful point of departure in coming to grips with issues of program evaluation and student growth.

Improve Managerial Skills

Steiss (1972) referred to effective public management as a complex and increasingly difficult task. The myriad sources of funds and variety of ways that funds can be expended make the fiscal manager's task a challenging one. In a student affairs division, it is highly likely that funds will become available through a variety of sources, including general institutional funds, auxiliary enterprises, federal sources, and gifts and endowments.

A general lack of expertise and experience characterizes many student affairs officers as budget managers (Pembroke, 1985). Many student affairs officers have come through academic disciplines that do not stress fiscal resource management, and others have not held positions that require a strong background in fiscal management. When faced with a complex budget, the student affairs officer is likely to face problems.

To rectify this situation, linkages need to be built between student affairs and the business affairs managers of the institution so that help can be obtained as needed. It may make sense for the division to hire a person with a strong financial background to serve as the budget manager. And, it also may be beneficial for the chief student affairs officer to focus his or her professional development activities for a period of time on resource management. If the student affairs officer cannot manage the budget effectively, ". . . inappropriate or a total lack of effective planning. . ." may result (Pembroke, 1985, pp. 101–102).

Maintain Flexibility

Another way the student affairs office might respond to the present financial environment in higher education is to approach resource allocation flexibly. The financial picture of an institution of higher education can change in a short period of time, often due to external factors such as the economy of the area served by the institution, dramatic changes in funds raised from gift and endowment sources, federal policy changes, and the like. Each of these factors, as well as other external and internal sources, will influence the student affairs budget.

Flexibility can include a response such as moving items from the institution's general fund to auxiliary sources. It might mean reallocating funds internally from one program area to another. Funds might be raised from external sources to support specific student programs and activities. The point is that continuing to do things because they were successful in the past is not an approach that will guarantee that the division will be able to meet its future obligations. Change for its own sake makes no sense, but trying to develop flexible and innovative approaches to solving fiscal problems will serve the division well in the future.

Practice Efficiency

At times there is fear in the higher education community that increased efficiency will entail losing something of our culture in the process. Institutions of higher education are not profit-making enterprises, and they do not have to satisfy their stockholders with increased dividends each quarter. On the other hand, they do need to satisfy their stakeholders that they are able to provide the best services, programs, and resources in exchange for the support they provide. Fecher (1985) observed that "The purposes of higher education are clear: teaching, research and public service. What is needed to deliver these purposes to their highest level of quality is effective (appropriate) and efficient (economical) use of the human and material resources available to colleges and universities" (p. 1).

Make Meaningful Comparisons

Often, student affairs falls into the trap of comparing itself with sister institutions to try to make the case that if it is underfunded compared with other institutions it will enjoy greater support. That can happen, but other forms of comparisons may be more useful.

One comparison that may be informative and useful is to examine how the proportion of the institution's budget with respect to student affairs has changed over a distinct period of time, such as the past 5 or 10 years. Has support for student affairs remained at about the same percentage over the years, or has the percentage declined? If it has declined, then it is possible to make the case that student affairs has been hurt more badly through budget retrenchment than academic affairs or other aspects of the institution's budget. It is one thing for budget cuts to be applied uniformly across all aspects of the institution, but quite another when student affairs has to shoulder more than its burden with respect to budget recessions. Indeed, Mortimer and Taylor (1984), in their survey of 318 chief academic officers (CAOs) of 4-year institutions, reported that there is significant tension between academic and nonacademic areas in resource allocation. In the survey, many of the CAOs indicated that academic affairs budgets had not been cut as severely as those of other areas on their campuses.

Another comparison worth examining is the extent to which support for student affairs functions from the institution's general fund (in the case of independent colleges, the tuition that students pay, and in the case of public institutions, tuition and state support) has been replaced by fees for service. If the institution has decided to finance student affairs through more user fees or grants and gifts, in effect institutional support has eroded and the analysis may be helpful in stopping this erosion. In this context reference is not being made to the traditional auxiliary service areas, such as housing and food service, but rather to such areas as the counseling service, which did not charge fees in the past, but may have to move in that direction to maintain a meaningful level of service to students and the campus community.

BUDGETING

"Making the budget process work has different connotations in different budgetary environments. In the higher education environment, it has different meanings depending on the type of institution, its organizational structure, its governance, its sources of revenue, and other important structural considerations" (Berg & Skogley, 1985, p. 1). The budget is the mechanism through which plans become undertakings (Lee & Van Horn, 1983).

All kinds of advice are available to those who are responsible for budgeting in higher education. In a tongue-in-cheek article on budget myths, Fincher (1986) pointed out that the reason the budgeting process is successful in higher education is that it has so many accommodating features. "Within hours after the arrival of a new fiscal year, budgeting-in-amendment begins" (p. 76). Nevertheless, there are some approaches to budgeting that have been utilized successfully in a variety of situations, and in this section, some of these will be identified and discussed within the context of managing the resources of the student affairs division.

Support the Institutional Mission

In developing a conceptual approach to the student affairs budget, it is wise to gear the budgetary plans of the student affairs division to the objectives of the academic departments and the institution as a whole (Robins, 1986). Pembroke (1985) explained that when allocations are made to the student affairs budget *after* requests of the academic departments have been satisfied, it is because the student affairs budget managers have not articulated how their divisional mission and goals contribute to and support the overall institutional mission. Pembroke cautions that fiscal decision makers need constant reminding of the significance of the student affairs division to the institution's mission and the essential contributions that student affairs makes to the fulfillment of that mission.

Astin (1985) characterized our present society as highly acquisitive; as a result, society often equates quality in higher education with institutional resources. Acquiring additional resources is one of the tasks that fall to chief student affairs officers, but success in acquiring new resources is not always easy. Pembroke (1985) wrote that the enhancement of new programs or the development of new initiatives will be successful only to the extent that the overall mission of the institution is enhanced by the additional funding. Keeping that observation in mind would be useful in considering general budgeting guidelines.

General Budgeting Guidelines

Pembroke (1985) identified five general budgeting guidelines that apply to the budget manager for the student affairs division. A brief discussion on each follows.

Know the guidelines. Most institutions develop a process for budgetary review that includes conferences with senior-level administrators or key faculty. In preparing for these conferences, certain guidelines are established for proposing new programs as well as maintaining present programs. The student affairs budget manager is advised to heed these guidelines and be well prepared for budget conferences. If the guidelines include sending material to various conferees 3 days in advance of the meeting, that should be done. If the guidelines require that budget managers are to ask for no more than 10% growth, they should not ask for more. When justification is required for special requests, it should be supplied. Although these suggestions are clear and almost simplistic, the budget request is likely to be in serious trouble even before the hearing if the suggestions are not heeded.

Know what is possible. Within the budgetary scheme, some things will be possible and others will not. If the institution is in the position of not being able to increase the number of staff for the student affairs division because of a steady state budget or an overall hiring freeze, it does no good to request an additional three positions. It never hurts to have new programs or ideas available upon request, but one has to be realistic in terms of what the institution can do with a budget request. Wildavsky (cited by Orwig & Caruthers, 1980) indicated that if an agency develops a pattern of submitting excessive budget requests, the funding organization will respond by reducing the budget even before the budget is examined in detail. On the other hand, LeLoup and Moreland (cited by Orwig & Caruthers) commented that the key to budget growth is acquiring political support to justify a large increase. They concluded that the best strategy is to come in ". . . as high as can be justified" (p. 353).

Observe deadlines. Earlier, the advisability of paying heed to the guidelines developed for budget preparation was stressed. Failure to do so will cause great problems for the budget manager. Other difficulties can occur when material is submitted late or in the wrong format. The entire institution's budget needs to be completed by a certain date in the right format, and the student affairs budget should not be a stumbling block for the budget office. By paying attention to the appropriate submission date and form, the student affairs budget officer will be doing the institution's budget office a favor and perhaps gaining the gratitude of that office by completing material correctly and on a timely basis. Earning the gratitude of the budget office may pay dividends at a later date.

Forecast problems. Through the budget process, the chief student affairs officer will have the opportunity to forecast problems. For example, if federal student financial aid monies will be distributed late because of a problem in Washington, the chief student affairs officer should anticipate the problem and recommend contingencies to solve it. As Ping noted, "the challenge is not to recognize problems but to recognize them in a timely fashion and with a will to address the issues they represent" (1986, p. 9). If the student affairs division is able to anticipate the influence of external forces on the institution, the perception that student affairs contributes to the institution's overall mission will be enhanced.

Respond to changing needs. "The goals of student services should not be considered separate from institutional goals; such services are not free-standing agencies with unrelated objectives of their own" (Kauffman, 1984, p. 25). There will be times when student affairs programs will need to be modified or perhaps eliminated as the nature of the student population or the institutional mission changes. "As in any organization, the budget and planning process should begin with an assessment of institutional needs" (Hyatt, 1985, p. 13). A simplistic example follows. Veterans' programs are not nearly as extensive today as they were 15 years ago because of changes in veterans' benefit programs and a shrinking number of military personnel, which has resulted in fewer veterans enrolling in institutions of higher education. On the other hand, the number of students older than the traditional age cohort of college students has increased. As a result, some chief student affairs officers have reduced veterans' programs on campus and increased expenditures for day-care programs. When the needs of the student body change, the student affairs program will need to be adjusted.

MAJOR ISSUES IN BUDGETING

Orwig and Caruthers (1980) listed three major issues related to the budgeting process. Each of these is manageable if the person responsible for the budget process understands the issues and utilizes the resources available to strike a reasonable compromise.

Technical Analysis Versus Political Negotiation

In viewing a budget one can take the position that it is nothing more than a technical document best left to accountants and financial managers. On the other hand, the budget is a "plan of action for the institution" (Meisinger & Dubeck, 1984, p. 5). As a result a balance needs to be struck between these two perspectives, which are not always complementary. Orwig and Caruthers (1980) concluded that technical approaches to budgeting are necessary adjuncts to decision making in an increasingly complex environment (p. 346). They predicted that institutional research would play an increasingly important role in providing support to the budget process. "Clearly, both politics and quantitative analysis have important roles in budgeting. Political negotiation provides a mechanism through which social and human values can be reflected in budgeting decisions. Quantitative analysis helps to refine options and explore the consequences of alternatives and thereby to inform negotiations" (p. 386). As a result, budgetary positions must be well-grounded not only in terms of how students are assisted or encouraged to develop, but also must be supported by appropriate technical expertise and command of the issues to make a solid contribution.

Competing Interests

At a minimum, students, faculty, and administrators all have an interest in an institution's budget, and their interests often compete. For example, student affairs administrators may desire to expand a program for students, but faculty may prefer to have the resources necessary for that program diverted to assist research projects. "Students are concerned about how well their own programs are supported financially" (Meisinger & Dubeck, 1984), and they want to have the very best faculty who, in turn, require competitive compensation for their work. Alumni and the community may have a stake in the institution's budget, and if it is state-supported, as Orwig and Caruthers pointed out, ". . . state agencies and legislators along with federal administrators must also be considered in the development of a budget" (1980, p. 347). That could be extended, again in the case of the state-assisted institution, to every citizen in the state because citizens' tax bills may be directly affected by the amount of support the state provides for its institutions of higher education. Orwig and Caruthers reduced the problems of participation to two competing forces—a desire for flexibility and the necessity for accountability. Budget managers and developers will have to balance these two competing interests. It is likely that this debate will not diminish over the next few years, and perhaps not for the foreseeable future. Balancing diverse interests is a major challenge to budget developers, according to Lee and Van Horn (1983).

Information Required

Orwig and Caruthers (1980) pointed to increasing costs related to the nature of the budgeting approach, the need for standard data definitions and procedures, and changes in budget formats. Although they agreed that these are formidable expenses of the budget process, they indicated that perhaps the real issue related to costs is to develop measures that examine the outcomes and performance of higher education. "Educational systems are not organized in such a way that provides information relevant to the development of production-function types of cost reporting procedures" (Lee & Van Horn, 1983, p. 21). That is an issue especially salient for student affairs administrators. As Kauffman (1984) pointed out, ". . . we must have the courage to know what quality is in our setting. If quality is anything determinate, we should know to distinguish its presence from its absence" (p. 31).

The standards published by the Council for the Advancement of Standards for Student Services/Development Programs (1986) are an excellent start in providing measures against which student affairs can compare its programs. But these need to be extended a step further to include regular reviews of programs, both external as well as internal, with student affairs' objectives to develop better ways to influence students' lives and growth.

Incremental Budgeting

As a point of definition, when we refer to the unit budget, what we mean is a departmental budget. For example, this might be the budget for the student housing department, the counseling center, or the department of judicial affairs. When unit budgets are aggregated, they form a divisional budget, referred to hereafter as the student affairs divisional budget.

Robins (1986) presented a particularly lucid discussion of unit budgeting. Much of what follows is based on this discussion. Unit budgets usually incorporate information from the previous fiscal year, and in preparing for the next fiscal year, the budget manager is asked to recommend expenditures for the coming year. Individual employees in the unit will be identified with their salary expenditures for the current budget year, and recommendations, to include actual dollars and percentage changes, will be made for the next fiscal year. The same will be true in general supply and expense categories, such as telephone, postage, and office supplies.

Guidelines normally are provided for the various budgeting categories. Salary increases that are permitted are given in a range (either in terms of a percentage or specific dollar amounts), and adjustments are provided for supplies, equipment, and travel. For example, postage may be expected to change 2%, telephone 10%, and salary adjustments typically range from 2% to 10%. The budget manager's tasks, then, are to apply the various adjustments to the supply and expense categories, and to make decisions about salary adjustments. This is more complicated in an environment where information about state legislative actions has been widely disseminated by the news media, for example, "State employees will receive average salary increases of 4.6% next year." One way to generate widespread dissatisfaction within a department's staff is to make salary adjustments using a process that staff do not understand. One approach to developing salary adjustments is to award cost-of-living increases to each employee, and to provide merit increments to those who perform exceptionally well. Salary changes will generate emotion on the part of employees, so the manager needs to be exceedingly careful in awarding increases.

Budget categories are identified in the unit budget in a variety of ways. These include: personal services, supplies, and expenses; personal services, wages, operations, travel, and capital; or personal services, supplies and operating expenses, and equipment. Few institutions use exactly the same categories, but basically the unit manager will be dealing with salaries and wages, operating costs, fringe benefits, equipment, and travel in some form.

Upon completing the unit budget, the manager will need to confer with the divisional manager to make sure that the proposal fits within the guidelines that the division has established for the various budget categories. No matter how careful the manager is in developing the unit budget, it is highly possible that the document will be modified in the institutional budget process. That is because budgeting is very much a function of institutional traditions and practices, historical accidents, and the availability of funds that can be used to accomplish the purpose of the institution (Fincher, 1986).

Historically, the line-item budget has been used in many institutions of higher education as their approach to unit budgeting. "The line item budget is a financial plan of expenditures expressed in terms of the kinds and quantities of objects to be purchased and estimated revenues needed to finance them during a specified period, usually one year. This budget generally includes the number of personnel employed by type of position" (Bubanakis, 1976, p. 8). The line-item budget, also known as the object budget, is designed to provide a balanced budget, where expenditures and revenues are equivalent, and it forces a regular review of activities and policies because the process is repeated annually (Bubanakis).

Building in the line-item approach is incremented budgeting, which is a time-tested approach of building next year's budget on last year's. "The weaknesses of incremental budgeting are also its strengths. It is simpler, easier to apply, more controllable, more adaptable, and more flexible than modern alternatives. . . . The fact that traditional incremental budgeting has endured while several budget innovations have had minimal success speaks to the strengths of the incremental approach" (Meisinger & Dubeck, 1984, p. 183).

"Implicit assumptions in the incremental budgeting approach are that the relative needs and priorities among organizational entities remain unchanged from one budget period to the next and that each item merely needs its proportionate share of any inflationary allowance" (Orwig & Caruthers, 1980, p. 355). Orwig and Caruthers were quick to point out, however, that as demographic changes alter the basic character of higher education, major reallocations will be needed. When that happens, incremental budgeting may be as burdensome as any other budgeting technique (p. 356). Nonetheless, that incremental budgeting has endured speaks to its strengths (Meisinger & Dubeck, 1984).

Other Budgeting Approaches

Methods other than the incremental and line-item approaches have been developed to address the budgeting process. Several are described briefly below.

Program budgeting. This approach to budgeting provides a more analytical approach than using line items. Steiss (1972) defined a program as ". . . a group of interdependent, closely related services or activities which possess or contribute to a common objective or set of allied objectives" (p. 157). "Program budgeting sets its sights on larger purposes, the objectives of an organization. These are stated in terms of available alternatives, which in turn are appraised in cost-benefit considerations" (Novick, 1973, p. 6). Instead of simply adjusting each line every year on the budget, the manager is forced to step back and look at the objectives of a particular program and determine the resources necessary to accomplish the program's objectives. If these objectives do not fit with the institution's mission, drastic changes in the budget may be in order. Or, the institution may be moving in a different direction, and as a result, will require more resources to be placed in support of a specific program because more students will be served. Robins (1986) pointed out that more emphasis is placed on considering costs in terms of benefits rather than dollars (p. 47). Suppose that an institution decided to focus on international education for its U.S. students. Assuming that the necessary services were not in place, support would have to be developed to assist students in study-abroad programs, and appropriate coursework in foreign languages and culture would have to be provided. Combining all these functions in planning a budget would be an example of program budgeting.

Planning, programming, budgeting systems (PPBS). This variation on program budgeting was developed by the Rand Corporation and later implemented by the Air Force and the Department of Defense. Some aspects of this approach have been utilized by institutions of higher education, such as setting objectives, grouping activities into programs designed to meet those objectives, identifying resources required by the programs, and measuring the effectiveness of the programs in meeting the objectives (Robins, 1986). "Planning and programming—a two step decision process—represent the substance of PPBS" (Hussain, 1976, p. 132). The process forces the budget developers to think about what they wish to accomplish in their various budget areas, to provide appropriate resources, and then to evaluate whether or not their objectives have been reached. "Compared with other budgeting practices, PPBS pays greater attention to developing and implementing a plan in making budget choices, has a multi-year rather than single-year time horizon, analyzes alternatives systematically, and relies on cost-benefit ratios to establish priorities and guide budget choices" (Orwig & Caruthers, 1980, p. 357).

The fundamental concepts of PPBS systems are not radically different from earlier program evaluation methods (Steiss, 1972). "The basic concept underlying program budgeting—presenting budgetary requests in terms of program 'packages' rather than in the usual line-item format—has been adopted as a central focus of the PPBS system. However, this concept has been broadened to encompass a structuring of programs according to objective regardless of agency responsibility" (Steiss, p. 154). Meisinger and Dubeck (1984) commented that PPBS has been more appealing on paper than in practice. PPBS has numerous disadvantages including defining what a program is (Meisinger & Dubeck) and measuring benefits and calculating cost-benefit ratios (Orwig & Caruthers, 1980). Hussain (1976) added that it is difficult to identify the outputs of higher education.

Zero-base budgeting. The zero-base budgeting system differs from the others in that the budget manager takes an entirely different conceptual approach. "Administrators must justify from base zero all of their departmental or agency budgeted expenditures. Nothing is taken for granted or simply continued at some previous level. Everything must be justified or discontinued through the use of cost benefit analysis" (Boyd, 1982, p. 430).

Harvey (1977) listed a number of advantages of zero-base budgets along with several disadvantages. Strengths of this approach are that it includes an annual program and expenditure review, develops cost-conscious staff, improves staff morale, and reduces empire building. On the other hand, Harvey indicated that zero-base budgeting increases paperwork, provides little motivation for staff to function properly, and demands more staff time (pp. 12–15).

An evaluation of the use of zero base budgeting by state universities in Texas indicated that this approach is no better or worse than the procedure used before (Boyd, 1982). Boyd concluded that the process requires reevaluation and considerable thought, which are desirable elements for any budgeting concept. Zero-base requires a great deal of time and paperwork. In addition, its use can make it difficult to reach agreement on priorities. Zero-base assumes no budget history and does not recognize continuing budgetary commitments, such as those to tenured faculty and key staff (Meisinger & Dubeck, 1984). Periodic program reviews may be more practical than moving to a zero-base approach (Meisinger & Dubeck).

Formula budgeting. According to Brinkman (1984), formula budgets are used in approximately half the states. The use of formulas goes back to 1951, and formula budgets tend to evolve even as they are employed; anything other than minor adjustments to the formulas on an annual basis seems to be the exception rather than the rule (Brinkman). One of the early problems with formula budgeting is that it was perceived as an allocation process rather than a resource document. What this suggests is that the formulas were perceived to be a means by which funds were dispensed rather than guidelines for planning. As a result mistrust was created among faculty administrators, legislators, and students (Berg & Skogley, 1985, pp. 1–2). "The basic intent of most formulas is to relate work load to appropriations. . ." (Brinkman, p. 23).

Stated succinctly, formula budgets tie the funding base for a particular activity to a mathematical equation. For example, the number of counselors in a counseling center may be determined by the number of students attending the institution, or the amount of money dedicated to a particular program area will be tied to the number of credit hours produced by that activity. Maw, Richards, and Crosby (1976) developed a monograph that explains in detail approaches to formula budgeting across an entire student affairs division.

According to Brinkman (1984), among the strengths of formula budgeting are that this approach enhances uniformity and ease of budget preparation; provides assistance in comparing across institutions, programs, and activities; routinizes the budget process; and provides for effective communication between budget developers and state-level budget decision makers. On the negative side, formula budgets tend to be based on past behavior, have a leveling effect on institutions and their quality, and may be rigid. New programs are at a disadvantage until they have developed a history (Meisinger & Dubeck, 1984). Brinkman recommended additional strategies to improve the formula budgeting process; these include providing incentives to managers, making the formulas more complex, and addressing the issue of quality. Kemper (1985) prepared a discussion on using a formula approach to allocating faculty. It provides useful reading for those interested in more details about formula budgeting.

Leslie (1984) offered several conclusions about formula budgets:

1. Past allocation is used to validate new formulas (p. 91).
2. This year's formula reflects last year's cost patterns (p. 91).
3. Where formulas are concerned, the politics are taken care of before the formula is adopted (p. 90).

Cost-center budgeting. Lee and Van Horn (1983) described the concept of cost-center budgeting, although they reported that it can be difficult to apply this concept across all the departments in an institution because some have much more of a service or support mission than do others (p. 189). Cost-center budgeting views every unit budget as self-supporting. That means that all costs generated by the department must be covered through tuition and fees, endowment income, fees for service, and the like. In effect, this approach treats academic units much in the way that auxiliary service units are conceived, and it is not very practical for the bulk of the institution. It works best, according to Meisinger and Dubeck (1984), in rather self-contained units, such as professional schools, and worst in units that provide service across the campus, such as the liberal arts college. Nonetheless, this is another way of approaching the budgeting process. Berg (1985) identified examples of this approach to budgeting.

Performance budgeting. Described as even less well-defined than other budgeting approaches (Orwig & Caruthers, 1980), this approach to budgeting resulted from the second era of reform in public administration (Lee & Van Horn, 1983). Performance budgeting was developed to improve work efficiency (Meisinger & Dubeck, 1984).

In the newer form of performance budgeting, resources (input) are related to activities (structure) and results (outcomes) (Meisinger & Dubeck, 1984). Outcomes are defined in both qualitative and quantitative terms. Expenditures are related to results. Orwig and Caruthers (1980) concluded that performance will be one criterion for determining where cutbacks may be made in higher education if an oversupply of opportunity develops. They also concluded, however, that performance budgeting in itself may not be an adequate budgeting methodology. Meisinger and Dubeck added that other problems with this approach include the following: performance measures have flowed from the state level down to institutions; quantitative measures have been used more often than qualitative measures; and outcome measures are often useless or controversial (p. 186).

CONCLUSIONS

This chapter has introduced the reader to the fiscal and budgetary environment of student affairs departments. This fiscal environment is challenging, and projections for the future are not optimistic. Although a variety of budgeting approaches are available, each has its strengths and weaknesses, and no approach emerges as clearly the preferred technique. Student affairs resource managers will be hard-pressed to maintain their base of support in the future, and will be able to do so only through careful management and prudent decisions.

REFERENCES

Astin, A.W. (1985). *Achieving educational excellence.* San Francisco: Jossey-Bass.

Berg, D.J. (1985). Getting individual and organizational goals to match. In D.J. Berg & G.M. Skogley (Eds.), *Making the budget process work* (pp. 65–78). New Directions for Higher Education No. 52. San Francisco: Jossey-Bass.

Berg, D.J., & Skogley, G.M. (1985). Editors' notes. In D.J. Berg & G.M. Skogley (Eds.), *Making the budget process work* (pp. 1–3). New Directions for Higher Education No. 52. San Francisco: Jossey-Bass.

Bowen, H.R. (1977). *Investment in learning.* San Francisco: Jossey-Bass.

Boyd, W.L. (1982). Zero-base budgeting: The Texas experience. *Journal of Higher Education, 53,* 429–438.

Brinkman, P.T. (1984). Formula budgeting: The fourth decade. In L.L. Leslie (Ed.), *Responding to new realities in funding* (pp. 21–44). New Directions for Institutional Research No. 43. San Francisco: Jossey-Bass.

Brown, R.D. (1987). Editorial. *Journal of College Student Personnel, 28,* 3.

Bubanakis, M. (1976). *Budgets.* Westport, CT: Greenwood.

Carnegie Council on Policy Studies in Higher Education. (1980). *Three thousand futures: The next twenty years for higher education.* San Francisco: Jossey-Bass.

Council for the Advancement of Standards for Student Services/Development Programs. (1986). *CAS standards and guidelines for student services/development programs.* N.p.: Author.

Evangelauf, J. (1986, August 6). College charges to students rising 6 pct. this fall. *The Chronicle of Higher Education,* pp. 1, 24.

Evangelauf, J. (1987, January 7). Students' borrowing quintuples in decade, raising the specter of a "debtor generation." *The Chronicle of Higher Education,* pp. 23, 28.

Farmer, J. (1979). Summary: The need for financial indicators. In C. Frances & S.L. Coldren (Eds.), *Assessing financial health* (pp. 85–87). New Directions for Higher Education No. 26. San Francisco: Jossey-Bass.

Fecher, R.J. (1985). Editor's notes. In R.J. Fecher (Ed.), *Applying corporate management strategies* (pp. 1–4). New Directions for Higher Education No. 50. San Francisco: Jossey-Bass.

Fincher, C. (1986). Budgeting myths and fictions. In L.L. Leslie & R.E. Anderson (Eds.), *ASHE reader on finance in higher education* (pp. 73–84). Lexington, MA: Ginn.

Frances, C. (1982). The financial resilience of American colleges and universities. In C. Frances (Ed.), *Successful responses to financial difficulty* (pp. 113–118). New Directions for Higher Education No. 38. San Francisco: Jossey-Bass.

Hansen, J.S. (1984). Reducing the burden of price. In L.H. Litten (Ed.), *Issues in pricing undergraduate education* (pp. 63–75). New Directions for Institutional Research No. 42. San Francisco: Jossey-Bass.

Harvey, L.J. (1977). *Zero-base budgeting in colleges and universities.* Littleton, CO: Ireland.

Hussain, K.M. (1976). *Institutional resource allocation models in higher education.* Paris: OECD.

Hyatt, J.A. (1985). Information: Setting the context for effective budgeting. In D.J. Berg & G.M. Skogley (Eds.), *Making the budget process work* (pp. 5–13). New Directions for Higher Education No. 52. San Francisco: Jossey-Bass.

Kauffman, J.F. (1984). Assessing the quality of student services. In R.A. Scott (Ed.), *Determining the effectiveness of campus services* (pp. 23–36). New Directions for Institutional Research No. 41. San Francisco: Jossey-Bass.

Kemper, G.A. (1985). Allocating faculty in the budgeting process. In D.J. Berg & G.M. Skogley (Eds.), *Making the budget process work* (pp. 31–45). New Directions for Higher Education No. 52. San Francisco: Jossey-Bass.

Kuh, G.D. (1979). Evaluation: The state of the art in student affairs. In G.D. Kuh (Ed.), *Evaluation in student affairs* (pp. 1–11). Cincinnati: ACPA.

Lee, S.M., & Van Horn, J.C. (1983). *Academic administration.* Lincoln: University of Nebraska Press.

Lenning, O.T. (1980). Assessment and evaluation. In. U. Delworth & G.R. Hanson (Eds.), *Student services: A handbook for the profession* (pp. 232–266). San Francisco: Jossey-Bass.

Leslie, L.L. (1984). Bringing the issues together. In L.L. Leslie (Ed.), *Responding to new realities in funding* (pp. 87–99). New Directions for Institutional Research No. 43. San Francisco: Jossey-Bass.

Maw, I.I., Richards, N.A., & Crosby, H.J. (1976). *Formula budgeting: An application to student affairs.* Washington, DC: ACPA.

McCorkle, C.O., Jr., & Archibald, S.O. (1982). *Management and leadership in higher education.* San Francisco: Jossey-Bass.

Meisinger, R.J., Jr., & Dubeck, L.W. (1984). *College and university budgeting.* Washington, DC: NACUBO.

Mooney, C.J. (1987, January 14). Some states seek big money, others just hope to avert reductions. *The Chronicle of Higher Education,* pp. 1, 26–32.

Mortimer, K.P., & Taylor, B.E. (1984). Budgeting strategies under conditions of decline. In L.L. Leslie (Ed.), *Responding to new realities in funding* (pp. 67–86). New Directions for Institutional Research No. 43. San Francisco: Jossey-Bass.

Novick, D. (1973). *Current practices in program budgeting.* London: Heineman.

Orwig, M.D., & Caruthers, J.K. (1980). Selecting budget strategies and priorities. In P. Jedamus & M.W. Peterson (Eds.), *Improving academic management* (pp. 341–363). San Francisco: Jossey-Bass.

Pembroke, W.J. (1985). Fiscal constraints on program development. In M.J. Barr and L.A. Keating (Eds.), *Developing effective student services programs* (pp. 83–107). San Francisco: Jossey-Bass.

Ping, C.J. (1986). Recognizing problems in state universities. In H. Hoverland, P. Mc-Inturff, & C.E. Topie Rohn, Jr. (Eds.), *Crisis management in higher education* (pp. 9–16). New Directions for Higher Education No. 55. San Francisco: Jossey-Bass.

Robins, G.B. (1986). From: Understanding the college budget. In L.L. Leslie & R.E. Anderson (Eds.), *ASHE reader in finance in higher education* (pp. 25–56). Lexington, MA: Ginn.

Steiss, A.W. (1972). *Public budgeting and management.* Lexington, MA: Heath.

CHAPTER 2

Private Versus Public Institutions: How Do Financial Issues Compare?

Donald B. Mills and *Margaret J. Barr*

Sound fiscal management skills are necessary for good student affairs administration. Student affairs managers and all those associated with higher education are faced with shrinking resources, increased demands, and new expectations for accountability. The issues that must be faced and the skills that must be mastered are remarkably similar in public and private institutions. There are, however, key differences between those two environments.

Fiscal management is often equated with budgeting. In fact, Mayhew (1979) indicated that "budgets are really a statement of educational purpose phrased in fiscal terms." (p. 54). Sound fiscal management is, however, more than the process of budgeting. It involves questions of funding sources, accountability patterns, response to external regulations, capital budgeting procedures, and long-range planning. In this chapter the similarities and differences regarding fiscal management issues between private and public institutions will be discussed. Many of these differences are a result of the legal organization and control of the institution.

LEGAL ISSUES

The power and authority for action in public institutions is derived from the statutory or constitutional entitlement of the institution. Authority to act in private institutions is based on the articles of incorporation, charter, or license of the institution. In both public and private institutions, power is vested in a governing board as an entity separate

21

from the individual members of the board. Any action taken by either a board member, or by officers or administrators of the institution in the name of the board, must be explicitly authorized by the governing body.

Public Institutions

A state may establish public institutions of higher education either as constitutionally autonomous entities or as statutory institutions. A constitutionally autonomous institution generally has increased protection from interference in institutional operations by other state agencies. In fact, the independence of constitutionally autonomous institutions has been upheld by the courts many times. (*Board of Regents of the University of Michigan v. Auditor General*, 1911; *Wall v. Board of Regents University of California*, 1940; and *State ex rel Peterson v. Quinlivan*, 1936). The constitutionally autonomous institution is, however, the exception rather than the rule. As Moos and Rourke (1979) indicated, "the greater part of law defining the status of higher education is legislative rather than constitutional." (p. 17).

Statutory institutions are created by the legislature and are subject to the control of the legislative body. Alexander and Solomon (1972) defined two types of statutory institutions. In the first type, the institution is organized as a primary agency and responds directly to the state legislature. Under second type, the institution is organized as a secondary agency and responds to the legislature through another intermediate agency. In addition, in some states a mixed reporting relationship is in effect, whereby the institution reports directly to the legislature on some matters and to a mid-level agency on others. The type of legal organization of the public institution will, in any case, define the rules, processes, and procedures for fiscal management.

Private Institutions

Private institutions, in general, have greater fiscal flexibility than do public institutions. Private institutions have limitations on power imposed by the charter or articles of incorporation. In addition, the power of the private governing board may also be limited by other state statutes or other laws of the state. For example, the "Sibley Hospital" case (*Stern v. Lucy Webb Hayes National Training School for Deaconesses and Missionaries*, 1974) defined the fiduciary responsibilities of trustees for endowment management and financial dealings. Thus, what may or may not be done in private institutions is directly related to the legal authority of the board and to other applicable state and federal laws. Examples of these laws are those related to charitable trusts, taxes, and unrelated business enterprises.

Each institution, whether public or private, develops a unique set of financial management protocols. These differ in private and public institutions primarily due to the sources of funds used to support the enterprise and the degree of autonomy of the institution.

In either setting the student affairs budget and the attendant financial management issues are very complex. "Although consuming typically less than five percent of an institution's overall budget, student affairs budgets rely on many sources of funds and thus raise unique fiscal management questions" (Pembroke, 1985, p. 68).

FUNDING SOURCES

Both private and public institutions depend on tuition, fees, room and board charges, grants, and fees for services to support student affairs units. Both public and private institutions also depend on endowment income and gifts for financial support, although private institutions are much more dependent on these sources of support. Public institutions receive their largest financial support from appropriated funds by the state legislature.

For student affairs these differences in funding sources have a great influence on financial management issues. The source of funds, as well as the restrictions on the use of those funds, make a big difference in operations.

Auxiliary Enterprises

In most institutions, revenue producing units such as housing, food service, athletics, and the student center are viewed as auxiliary enterprises. Any unit that generates all or a large part of its operating budget from sales or services is usually classified in this category.

In public institutions, these units are usually expected to be self-sustaining, and all direct and indirect costs associated with the unit are charged back to the unit. Support from appropriated funds is usually minimal. Excess income over expenditures is returned to an auxiliary reserve and designated for long-term repair, renovation, capital improvements, or operating budget deficits.

Auxiliary enterprises in private institutions are not necessarily viewed as self-sustaining. Income generated through such services may be viewed as part of the general income stream of the institution. In turn, auxiliaries often receive budget support from the university in the form of utility subsidies or absorption of indirect costs. Excess income over expenses under these circumstances is generally used as a general budget-supporting device or returned to a general university reserve. The auxiliaries do not have exclusive use of excess income and must make their case with other units for long-range projects and capital improvements.

Each approach to funding of auxiliaries has merit. It is important, however, that the student affairs manager understand the rules and the expectations within the environment.

Fees for Service

There has been a growing trend, particularly in public institutions, to move toward charging a fee for specific services in such units as health centers and counseling centers. This approach to funding has emerged in response to the need for increased revenue and a philosophy that users of a service should pay the entire cost for that service. If it becomes the prime budget support mechanism, this approach has great potential problems. Often the students most in need of services are reluctant to access them on a fee basis. As part of a budget support strategy, charging fees for specialized services can have merit. It needs, however, to be used judiciously.

Student Fees

Substantial support for student affairs units in both private and public institutions comes from student fees. Usually a general student fee is assessed for all students and proportionately distributed to the units. Differences arise between public and private institutions not only in the process of setting such fees but also on the upper limitations of a fee. In public institutions, either through legislative mandate or institutional practice, setting and distributing fees usually is a complex process. Students are highly involved in the process, and elaborate fee review processes are the norm. In that type of environment, the student affairs manager must be prepared to defend each line item in the budget and articulate needs in a clear and concise manner.

In private institutions, the establishment and distribution of fees is usually an administrative matter. Fees are considered part of the total income stream of the institution rather than a designated budget support mechanism for certain units. Justification for budgets still is required; however, the process usually is less influenced by external political forces.

In both private and public institutions, fees are an important source of support for student affairs units. Approval in both institutional types for changes in fees usually must be given by the governing board of the institution.

Budget Appropriations

General revenue budget support is crucial to student affairs units in both public and private institutions. The differences lie in the source of those funds. Endowment income, gifts, and tuition provide the prime source of revenue in private institutions. Public institutions rely on appropriated funds from the state legislature in addition to the sources listed for independents.

The budgeting process flows from the source of the funds, with public institutions having to meet deadlines, rules, and procedures mandated by other state agencies, the legislature, and their own governing board. In private institutions, internal rules and regulations prevail. Either environment requires that the student affairs manager understand the rules, follow the procedures, and meet all applicable deadlines.

Fiscal management is not an isolated set of processes. Sound fiscal management requires accountability to appropriate decision makers and constituency groups.

ACCOUNTABILITY

The knowledgeable student affairs administrator recognizes the need for accountability to various constituent groups in program offerings and effectiveness. Furthermore, that recognition includes acknowledging that these constituent groups can provide either support or challenge to the management of student affairs. Fiscal issues and fiscal management often bring the agendas and concerns of specific constituency groups into sharp focus.

For some constituent groups, there is interest in the allocation of resources for specific programs in which they hold interest. Examples include funding for child care, athletic support, or minority programming. Other constituency groups such as trustees, faculty, and staff are concerned that funds be adequate to meet institutional goals and be handled in a responsible manner. Still other constituents such as alumni and donors consider the public perception of institutional activities a primary focus. Finally, a number of constituent groups such as students, faculty, and administrators reflect interests that are more universal, spanning specific programs, responsible fiscal management, and perception of the institution.

To be appropriately accountable, the student affairs administrator must accomplish three objectives. First, programs and services must be clearly related to institutional objectives and goals. Second, the manager must prove that proposed program outcomes are appropriate and consistent with institutional goals. Finally, the administration must ensure that effective financial management controls (both budgeting and expenditures) are in place and are used to evaluate program effectiveness.

It is essential that performance be related to financial management. Berg (1985) indicated:

> Even though the performance of universities and their subunits is extremely difficult to measure or even approximate, the total dissociation of resource allocation and performance measurement would be the ultimate incentive mistake. Like it or not, the resources of an institution are a function of what its clientele perceive as its performance. (p. 75)

Thus, it is essential that constituent groups and their interests be identified. Mere recognition and identification of constituency groups is not enough, however. The specific concerns of each constituency group must also be precisely defined and recognition given to the reality that agendas of diverse constituency groups may be in conflict.

Public Institutions

The groups with the greatest long-term influence on public institutions are those political bodies providing the primary basis of institutional support. These typically include state legislatures, coordinating boards and, in the case of community colleges, local governing boards. Student affairs administrators most often act in concert with other institutional administrators in working with these bodies. Because of the political nature of these bodies, strategies must be devised to present information in a useful and clear manner. Information for these groups should include the results of previous funding as well as future needs. Specific information focusing on both program and fiscal outcomes is appropriate and helpful to these key decision makers.

The largest constituent group and the most immediately present is students. Students are frequently major decision makers in terms of spending student fee revenues and are consumers of many programs and services offered by student affairs organizations. Students play an important part in the fiscal success of a student affairs organization. The student affairs administrator must be sensitive to student concerns and ensure that available funds are used to meet the needs of the greatest possible number of students. When financial support for an operation rests on direct funding for student fees, or if raises in general tuition and fees are not understood by students, then controversy can result. Nonproductive controversy actually can result in poor decisions and lack of fiscal support. Special caution should be taken when raising student fees, room and board charges, or health center fees to ensure that students are aware of the needs for increases and that they support the increases.

Governing boards frequently are very close to campus programs and may have special interests in student affairs. The astute administrator will be certain that board members are well informed and understand the major goals of student affairs. This will be of special assistance when a specific controversy threatens to influence perceptions of an entire program. When this occurs, funding may be jeopardized inappropriately. Having clearly stated program goals and outcomes as well as clearly stated financial results as they relate to goals and outcomes is a necessary part of the relationship with boards.

Other important constituent groups include accrediting agencies, parents, and citizens groups. In each of these instances, a sensitivity to how these groups perceive campus decisions is crucial. The clear relationship of financial resources and management to institutional goals and programs must be evident to these groups. Their involvement often is irregular but can be crucial to a successful student affairs organization.

Private Institutions

The constituent groups that affect private institutions are similar to those that affect public institutions but vary in their emphasis. The critical constituent groups are less likely to be governmental agencies, but are more likely to be students, parents, and governing boards. The common thread between public and private institutions is that primary constituent groups also are major sources of institutional funding.

Although parent groups are an important constituency for public institutions, in private institutions sensitivity to parents is required in order to ensure long-term success. Parents exercise an influence similar to a consumer in a retail business. Student affairs policies, priorities, and programs are influenced by parental expectations. Fees and other charges are more directly related to perceived value in all areas of private institutions, including student affairs, than in public institutions. Because of the consumer orientation in private institutions, outcome assessment and relationship to cost are important decision variables for parents.

Students in private institutions, as a constituent group, function in a manner similar to students in public institutions. However, students in private institutions may make demands based on the cost of the institution including tuition, fees, and incidental charges. This financial relationship may lead to unrealistic expectations that personal concerns be satisfied without regard for broader policy considerations.

Because enrollment plays a significant role in funding for private institutions, it may necessitate that financial decisions be made, at least in part, with an eye to the short-term as well as long-term enrollment effects. The demographic characteristics of private institutions also will provide a partial basis for financial decisions as they relate to expectations and perceived quality. Thus, services and facilities in private institutions may prove to be more sensitive to student input than might be the case in public institutions.

The governing boards in private institutions serve as a constituent group in much the same manner as in public institutions. However, two important differences will affect the student affairs administrator. Boards are generally self-selecting rather than appointed through a political process, and board members frequently have had a prior involvement with the institution. An awareness of these factors assists the student affairs administrator to focus on institutional costs and financial management. It is realistic to expect that a student affairs administrator will not experience volatility in board members and will experience a consistency of board policy and behavior. Long-term planning is facilitated in this type of environment.

A constituent group unique to private institutions, particularly to church-related institutions, is the sponsoring agency. Sponsoring agencies frequently will have a specific philosophical point of view that requires programmatic and policy decisions. From a financial point of view this influences the allocation of funds and frequently the reporting of financial results. Priorities may be established that necessitate adherence to sponsoring agency interest to the exclusion or limitation of the priorities of other constituent groups. Sensitivity to sponsoring agency interests must be balanced against other interests. Potential financial implications of decisions that run counter to sponsoring agency interests must be clearly defined and articulated.

Private institutions also must be aware of the requirements of accrediting bodies in ways that are similar to public institutions. Ultimately this means that programs are offered that meet institutional objectives and are supported by appropriate financial allocations.

Governments have less influence on private than public institutions in fiscal matters. However, because state charters are issued to private institutions, some requirements for reporting data (financial and otherwise) and for program approval (with corresponding financial obligations) may be required. Neither private nor public institutions are immune from external regulations.

EXTERNAL REGULATIONS

The involvement of external regulators extends throughout the entire scope of financial management, ranging from program demands to personnel costs. The need, of course, exists for the student affairs administrator to be aware of the regulations, to measure their effect, and to maximize the positive opportunities offered by the situation.

Program Considerations

Frequently, state agencies or officials will mandate that certain programs be offered. Mandates may take the form of programs in academic assistance to underprepared students or specific services offered to handicapped students. In any case, the effect of mandated programs is threefold. First, funds must be made available to conduct the program; second, facilities must be made available to house the program; and third, staff must be assigned to design and implement the program. Depending on the availability of funds from the imposing agency, the mandated program will, to a greater or lesser extent, change institutional program priorities and department responsibilities.

An additional concern that student affairs administrators face is the proper allocation of funds to specific programs. By law, certain types of funds may be used only to fund certain types of programs. For example, it may be impermissible to use student fees to support auxiliary service enterprises in a public institution. Likewise, financial support for some functions may require that specific fees be levied for that purpose.

The approval process for fees also may be regulated externally. For example, in many public institutions the use of student fees as a means of funding programs requires approval of the student body in a referendum. In addition, the state may legislate fee ceilings that may not be exceeded regardless of student or administrative inclination.

Personnel

External regulations can play an important role in staffing patterns, salaries, and benefits. Frequently, public institutions are required to account for funds using specific procedures. Similarly, allocations of funds may require mandated procedures. The result of these regulations may influence staffing by increasing administrative overhead. This, then, has the potential to diminish the number of staff available for direct program implementation.

Salary schedules in public institutions are externally determined when a classification system is used for student affairs employees. These schedules may be civil service classifications or be imposed through union agreements. In either case, flexibility is lessened in determining initial salaries and annual increases. Certain situations also may develop that make it difficult to change a staffing assignment or relieve staff of their present position.

Finally, fringe benefits must be paid to all staff. The amount is generally established as a percentage of salary. In both public and private institutions, the fringe benefit package is established outside the division of student affairs. In public institutions the amount most often is established at the level of a state agency. When the fringe benefit percentage is constant and relatively stable, then the planning for this expense is not difficult. In periods of tight budgets, however, the charges for fringe benefits may revert from an institutional or state level to a departmental level without a corresponding increase in funding. This could result in up to a 30% decline in funds available for delivery of programs and services. Fringe benefits are a hidden but crucial expense item that should be carefully scrutinized by financial managers.

Differences in Public and Private Institutions

Because most external regulations are imposed by state agencies, the effects are felt primarily by public institutions. Changes in law, procedures, and state education policy have little effect on private institutions. However, private institutions are not immune to the actions of governmental bodies. If a state provides financial aid funds to citizens who attend private schools, then these funds are subject to regulation and, perhaps, change in support. Collection and reporting of statistical data frequently are required of private and public institutions alike. There are, of course, financial requirements to support the data collection effort.

External regulations directed by governmental bodies to public agencies have no effect on private institutions. Thus, issues discussed above such as fringe benefits or salary requirements that are state mandated affect state institutions. However, regulations promulgated by unions, or accrediting agencies, would have similar effects on public and private institutions alike.

External factors can influence both the operating budget and the long-term capital budget of the institution. Planning for capital expenditures, independent of the issue of external regulation, is a most difficult task.

CAPITAL BUDGETING

Recently, a report from the Republic of China indicated that student residence construction was averaging $6.50 per square foot. That low-cost figure for construction would be most welcome in any institution of higher education in the United States. Here, both public and private institutions face major expenditures for any new construction and also face massive expenditures to cover deferred maintenance of buildings. In fact, the National Association of College and University Business Officers indicates that the costs associated with deferred maintenance are the biggest fiscal issue higher education faces today (Pembroke, 1985).

In either public or private institutions, financing new construction or major repairs and renovations requires unique planning and budgeting protocols. Usually, such capital expenditures are funded from different sources, are budgeted separately, and require financing plans spanning several fiscal years. The philosophy of the institution regarding long-term debt, the status of current physicial facilities, and the institution's approach to financial planning all will influence the capital budgeting process.

There are four major approaches to funding capital expenditures: loans, bonds, self-financing, and gifts. The methods used will reflect the financial philosophy of the institution and the legal parameters on institutional actions. Public institutions frequently use loans or sell bonds for capital budget items. Private institutions are more apt to rely on self-financing or major gifts, although all methods are used by all types of institutions.

Loans

The most popular form of loans are government programs for specific categories of construction such as housing, libraries, science facilities, or energy conservation. Such programs have the advantage of low interest rates and long amortization periods. Under such programs, a limited fund pool is established, and the institution must apply for and show need for the funds. Debt repayment either is built into the total operating budget of the institution, or in the case of auxiliaries, from revenue generation. These programs have assisted in financing much of the new construction on campuses. Despite their obvious advantages, loans do require mortgaging the future to pay for the present, and institutions must meet certain government requirements in order to participate. These restrictions make such loan programs unattractive to many private institutions.

Another approach is to borrow money for construction, repair, and renovation from private lending institutions. Marketplace rates will prevail, so the advantage of low interest is lost. There are not, however, as many restrictions as with government programs, and that is seen as an advantage by some private schools.

Bonds

By far the most popular form of financing for public institutions is to issue bonds. Future revenue in the form of student fees, user fees, or room rentals is pledged to pay back the bondholders. Amortization periods are usually 20 to 30 years, and debt service can be spread out. The institution must meet the legal requirements for the sale of tax-free bonds and gain a credit rating from Standard and Poors or Moody.

Bonds are used less frequently in private institutions due to disclosure requirements and concern with financing long-term debt. Also, other alternatives are available to many private institutions that are not as readily available in the public sector.

Self-Financing

Three alternatives are available under a self-financing option. Alternative one is to establish a reserve or repair and renovation fund through yearly appropriations. This fund is then used to finance major repairs and renovations, and repayment schedules are established through the operating budget. Alternative two is to borrow from the endowment and repay the amount borrowed over a set time period. This option has the disadvantage of reducing revenue through loss of endowment interest over the period of the loan. The third alternative requires that an endowment be set up for the potential repair, maintenance, and operational costs for each newly constructed building. This alternative requires more capital at the construction phase but does not provide resources for long-term problems. Alternative one is extensively employed in both private and public institutions. Alternative two is rarely employed in public institutions but is an option chosen by many independents. Alternative three is used more often in private institutions to combat massive maintenance costs.

Gifts

A gift to pay for the entire cost of a new building, for portions of a building, or for major renovation of existing facilities is one of the easiest ways to finance capital expenditures. Gift support also requires a great deal of work in locating potential donors and matching their desires with those of the institution. Gift support needs to be carefully managed to avoid donor control of the project and implementation of programs. Usually these problems can be solved with careful attention to detail and involvement of key decision makers. Private institutions traditionally have relied on gift support for capital expenditures. Except in major public universities, this approach to funding has been relatively untapped in the public sector.

Whatever the approach to capital budgeting, the student affairs administrator must be aware of the decision protocols and limitations in the process. Understanding is the first step in effective fiscal management. Tools are available to aid the process of understanding. The next section describes one such tool.

RATIO ANALYSIS

For the student affairs administrator, ratio analysis serves as a useful tool in two ways. First, a comparison can be made between past and present performance. Second, ratios can be used to project future financial performance. The appropriate use of ratio analysis provides a methodology that is effective in evaluating services and programs.

The purpose behind ratio analysis is deceptively simple. The intent is to provide an overview of a program's financial health with a minimum of detail (Minter et al. 1982). The following questions can then be asked regarding the financial affairs of a program or service:

- Is the program healthy?
- Is the program in a financially better position than previously?
- Did the program live within its means during the period under discussion?
- Why did financial ratios behave as they did?

The above questions are in response to what has happened in the past. After determining answers to historical questions, a future orientation can be assumed. When one examines the future, the following questions can be asked:

- What program changes will cause the ratios to change?
- What consequences will accrue if the changes are installed?

Ratio analysis, then, will allow the student affairs administrator to make judgments about a program's financial health and the financial effect of changes to a program. Furthermore, programs that use similar financial ratios can then be compared and decisions for future funding can be made.

Types of Ratios

The choices of ratios generally are decisions best made locally by institutions, and they are dependent on local interests and needs. Some types of ratios are statements of (1) the relationship between costs and the number of students involved in a program, (2) the relationship between costs and facility size, (3) the relationship between net revenues and total revenues, (4) the relationship between specific program expenses and total available funds, and (5) the relationship between revenues and number of students.

These might, for example, be used to indicate that a particular program provides a greater return to the institution in terms of cost per student than another program. The ratio would be:

$$\frac{\text{costs}}{\text{\# of students.}}$$

If program A costs $1,000 and serves 100 students, the ratio would be

$$\frac{\$1,000}{100} = \$10/\text{student.}$$

If program B costs $1,500 and serves 200 students, the ratio would be

$$\frac{\$1,500}{200} = \$7.50 \text{ per student.}$$

Assuming that programmatically each approach produced the same desired result, then program B would be selected as more cost-efficient. In other situations, the cost per student could be evaluated year to year to ensure continuing program effectiveness.

Year-to-year forecasting of costs is especially helpful when looking at costs of facility operation. If a ratio is established for facility management such as

$$\frac{\text{expenses}}{\text{total square feet}},$$

then the results of this ratio can be used to predict needed revenues from year to year. The changes in expenses will alter results. These must in turn be evaluated not only in terms of increased expenses per foot but also in terms of improved or decreased performance.

It should always be remembered that ratio analysis will provide only a financial statement of program effectiveness of results. These must then be evaluated against program or service goals in order to be of assistance in decision making.

Differences Between Public and Private Institutions

The use of ratio analysis does not depend upon governing structures for their use. Typically, ratios will be established as they have meaning for administrators. Certain ratios, however, may have specific needs for public institutions such as mandated reserves for bond retirement, which could be stated as

$$\frac{\text{reserves}}{\text{total revenues}} = X\%.$$

The percent in this case could be a mandated percentage.

Formula funding is a specific type of ratio that many states use to fund institutions. Formula funding provides a method for states to support funding to institutions. For example, a legislative body may indicate that it will provide $2.00 per student for general administration of the institution. The ratio would be stated as amount/student X number of students = total revenues. To increase revenues, therefore, either the funds per student or the number of students must increase.

Formula funding also may be used to implement specific programs. For example, a legislative body may indicate that special programs for disadvantaged students will be part of state institution program offerings. To motivate institutions to provide these programs, a formula such as funds/disadvantaged students X number of disadvantaged students = total program funds could be used. Because of the nature of the process, the creation of the formula amounts becomes the critical part of analysis.

Implementation

A ratio analysis system of financial management is a tool that does not need to be adopted by an entire institution or even an entire division to be effective. Individual departments will find the tool useful. Ratio analysis has utilitarian value in establishing budgets, establishing new programs, and evaluating programs in times of budget cuts. Any budget manager may create ratios found to be useful. Thus a placement office may establish a series of ratios such as:

- $\dfrac{\text{cost of placement of specific majors}}{\text{cost of total placement of students}}$

- $\dfrac{\text{cost of career fair}}{\text{\# of students involved}}$ or $\dfrac{\text{cost of printed career materials}}{\text{\# of students using materials}}$

- $\dfrac{\text{cost of computer-assisted guidance}}{\text{\# of students assisted}}$ or

- $\dfrac{\text{cost of counselor guidance}}{\text{\# cost of students assisted}}$

In the above example, the resulting ratios will assist in determining where additional efforts or funds should be placed. The use of ratio analysis assists the student affairs administrator in determining the most cost-effective methods to meet program goals.

A CASE EXAMPLE

"State U" is an institution that is part of a system governed by a board of regents appointed by the governor. "Private U" is a private institution governed by a self-perpetuating board. Staff members at both institutions are interested in developing a substance abuse program. Interested staff have completed a needs assessment, developed a program plan, and projected the fiscal resources necessary to implement the program. Total costs for personnel, equipment, and supplies are estimated to be $250,000 in both institutions. At both institutions funds are not available in the current operating budget of the division of student affairs to support the new program initiative. New funds must be secured.

Step One is the same at both institutions. Staff members must convince the chief student affairs officer (CSAO) that the project has merit and should be supported as part of the divisional budget request.

Step Two is also similar if the CSAO supports the program. The new program is prioritized with other above-base-line budget requests from the division.

Step Three requires the CSAO to request support for the new program through reallocation of institutional resources. If that process is successful, the issue is resolved. If it is not, the processes begin to diverge between the public and private institution.

Private Institution Approach

Usually above-base-line budget requests for the entire institution are identified as part of the budget process. The amount of new revenue needed to support these requests is projected. Negotiations then begin to determine what new revenue sources are possible given the current economic climate. Once the pool of dollars from new revenue sources is determined, the institutional list of above-base-line budget requests is examined, and requests are matched to revenue sources. Three outcomes are possible: The new project will be funded at the requested level, a reduced allocation for the new project is given, or the project is not funded. The process is internal to the institution and requires the CSAO to have critical and detailed information in order to make decisions as part of the total budget process.

Public Institution Approach

Depending on the state, a number of scenarios are possible. The institutional priority for the new program is determined. If it becomes a priority, it is submitted as part of the budget process to the system office and the governing board. The request may be reduced prior to submission or at the system level. It also may not receive support at the system level and be removed from the total budget request. If the legislature uses a line-item approach to funding, the request must again be justified at the legislative committee level. Finally, even if the program survives (or if part of it survives) legislative review, it may not receive support at the gubernatorial level.

If the program is supported, other state regulations come into play, including approval for positions, classification of positions, and regulations on the expenditure of funds. The process of fiscal support for the new program is much more complicated at the state institution. Whatever the environment, however, understanding the budget decision-making process is critical.

SUMMARY

Although there are many commonalities, the process of budgeting and managing fiscal resources differs between public and private institutions. These differences stem from the source of funds used to support the enterprise, the amount of external control exercised in fiscal management, and the overall budget philosophy of the institution. In both environments, an understanding of established budget procedures, protocols, and decision-making structures is essential. Student affairs administrators clearly must develop skills in fiscal management and understand the political dimensions of the decision-making process. To do less will ensure that the student affairs division will not receive necessary and sufficient support to meet student and institutional needs.

REFERENCES

Alexander, K., & Solomon, E. (1972). *College and university law*. Charlottesville, VA: Michie.

Berg, D. (1985). Getting individual and organizational goals to match. In D.J. Berg and G.M. Skogley (Eds.), *Making the budget process work* (pp. 65–78). San Francisco: Jossey-Bass.

Mayhew, L. (1979). *Surviving the eighties: Strategies and procedures for solving fiscal and enrollment problems*. San Francisco: Jossey-Bass.

Minter, J. & Others. (1982). *Ratio analysis in higher education*. New York: Peat Marwich Mitchell.

Moos, M., & Rourke, F. (1979). *The campus and the state*. Baltimore: Johns Hopkins.

Pembroke, J. (1985). Fiscal constraints on program development. In M. Barr and L. Keating (Eds.), *Developing effective student services programs* (pp. 83–106). San Francisco: Jossey-Bass.

LEGAL CASES

Board of Regents of the University of Michigan v. Auditor General, 132 N.W. 1037 (Mich. 1911).

State ex rel Peterson v. Quinlivan, 268 N.W. 858 (Minn. 1936).

Stern v. Lucy Webb Hayes National Training School for Deaconesses and Missionaries, 381 F. Supp. 1003 (D.D.C. 1974).

Wall v. Board of Regents University of California, 102 P. 2d 533 (Ct. of App. Cal. 1940).

CHAPTER 3

Trends in Management Information Systems for Student Affairs Officers

Jerry R. Quick

No other technological advance has boosted personal productivity as much as microcomputers. Clearly they have increased work output, unleashed creativity, reduced redundant clerical work and, in general, made life more enjoyable and pleasant for those in the work force who must manipulate financial data, generate and produce correspondence, and use databases.

Many business executives and university managers report such results. One company, Northern Telecom, Inc., indicated that the use of microcomputers increased the productivity of at least 50% of their staff by an average of 3 hours per day.

Perhaps one of the most significant trends in the field is the use of microcomputers as an intelligent link to campus mainframes. This link enables a student affairs administrator to pull information from the mainframe and use a personal computer to manipulate the information with a spreadsheet or database program.

A Current Example of Computer Use in Student Affairs

Table 1 summarizes part of the information from a 1986 survey of computer uses in collegiate housing, food service, conference services, and other related areas conducted by Morris Welch, Associate Director of Residential Housing at Louisiana State University, for the Association of College and University Housing Officers—International. Although it certainly is not an exhaustive list of all applications found under the student affairs umbrella, it is illustrative of the management information trends in this large segment of student services.

TABLE 1
Housing and Food Service Functions Performed on Computers
(No. Reporting = 214)

Applications	Micro	Mini	Main	O/L	Batch	Prop	New
Conference Housing (134 out of 214)							
Store Reservations/ Assignments	43	14	39	38	13	9	36
Prepare Billings	23	14	49	34	19	6	21
Operate Desks	14	3	7	7	1	3	12
Record/Reconcile Cashiering Activities	17	9	37	25	6	2	14
Generate Desk Work Schedules	12	2	1	2	0	1	7
Generate Cleaning Schedules	16	2	4	3	2	1	8
Publish Rosters	51	18	47	32	19	8	35
Print Name Tags	19	6	10	7	2	3	13
Store Historical Occupancy/ Financial Data	45	10	40	27	15	10	26
Prepare Statistical Reports	45	12	29	21	13	12	28
Maintain Promotional Mailing List	31	13	30	15	8	5	18
Applications/Assignments (193 out of 214)							
Store/Report Space Inventory	36	23	99	70	40	14	45
Store/Report Single Applicant/Occupant Data	43	27	111	87	38	15	46
Store/Report Family Applicant/Occupant Data	18	8	56	36	22	5	17
Match Roommates by Defined Criteria	19	8	40	27	22	7	20
Assign Applicants to Rooms/ Apartments	18	14	64	48	26	10	26
Maintain Waiting Lists	35	15	37	31	14	9	31
Publish Rosters	45	27	123	58	68	16	42
Store/Report Historical Appl'n/Occup'y Data	41	20	74	39	32	14	36
Analyze Application/ Occupancy/Demand Trends	42	13	34	18	12	8	26

TABLE 1 (*continued*)
Housing and Food Service Functions Performed on Computers
(No. Reporting = 214)

Applications	Micro	Mini	Main	O/L	Batch	Prop	New
Word Processing/ Correspondence (170 out of 214)							
Issue Personalized Correspondence (merge file)	107	32	37	28	14	26	42
Assemble Documents (from prewritten paragraphs)	102	28	26	22	6	19	33
Prepare Reports (text, tables, graphs, etc.)	110	24	23	23	4	19	37
Prepare Newsletters	85	20	12	15	2	12	26
Prepare Advertisements/ Signs/Banners	59	9	11	9	1	6	15
Financial Assessment (183 out of 214)							
Store Accounts Receivable File	18	26	133	74	53	12	27
Calculate/Assess Rental Charges	22	19	104	62	41	9	30
Calculate/Assess Standard Damage/Misc Charges	16	17	66	46	24	6	20
Prepare Rent Billings	16	23	110	41	64	11	27
Prepare Damage/ Miscellaneous Billings	21	17	75	41	32	7	28
Record/Reconcile, Refund Reservation Deposits	17	20	100	55	45	12	26
Budgeting/Reporting (163 out of 214)							
Store/Reconcile Current Financial Data	54	23	103	42	47	14	27
Prepare Current Financial Reports	51	21	81	30	39	11	30
Analyze Cost Data	52	18	41	17	17	8	22
Determine Rental Rates	52	11	11	10	4	5	18
Store Historical Financial Data	46	15	74	21	26	12	23
Prepare Historical Financial Reports	48	14	52	18	20	10	20
Analyze Financial Trends	55	13	21	10	7	6	20

TABLE 1 (*continued*)
Housing and Food Service Functions Performed on Computers
(No. Reporting = 214)

Applications	Micro	Mini	Main	O/L	Batch	Prop	New
Student Development (128 out of 214)							
Compile Program/Activity Interest Surveys	38	13	32	14	19	4	19
Prepare/Maintain Program/ Activity Calendar	27	7	5	5	1	2	14
Evaluate Programs/Activities	20	5	7	2	5	1	11
Maintain Resident Disciplinary Records	30	8	7	9	0	4	17
Maintain/Reconcile Student Government Accounts	20	8	33	9	14	1	12
Generate Student Development Transcripts	9	5	20	8	8	0	5
Compile/Catalog Resource Files	15	5	9	3	2	1	8
Access Self-Administered Advising Programs	7	3	4	1	2	2	6
Access Library Catalog From Living Areas	2	2	8	5	1	1	2
Off-Campus Housing (68 out of 214)							
List Apartments/Rooms	39	7	16	12	4	2	11
List Roommates	21	4	11	10	3	3	8
Assist Tenant/Landlord Mediation	3	2	1	1	0	0	2
List Commuter Rides/Riders	5	3	3	2	1	1	1
Food Service (107 out of 214)							
Prepare Menus	32	16	6	6	4	6	15
Inventory/Reorder Foodstuffs	36	20	15	12	7	5	16
Monitor/Control Meal Access	34	41	5	11	3	10	10
Report/Analyze Meal Usage Data	43	41	8	13	5	11	15
Generate Employee Work Schedules	13	7	2	1	1	0	5
Maintenance/Housekeeping (121 out of 214)							
Inventory/Issue Keys	26	9	8	6	3	5	19
Inventory/Reorder Supplies	31	6	9	8	4	3	18

TABLE 1 (*continued*)
Housing and Food Service Functions Performed on Computers
(No. Reporting = 214)

Applications	Micro	Mini	Main	O/L	Batch	Prop	New
Inventory Equipment/ Appliances/Furnishings	31	8	41	14	19	7	23
Maintain Room Condition Inventory	15	3	5	4	1	1	12
Issue/Track Maintenance Orders	38	11	20	12	8	3	24
Issue/Track Requisitions/ Bids/Orders/Delivery	29	10	24	17	9	4	20
Generate Preventive Maintenance Schedules	23	4	5	4	2	0	12
Generate Employee Work Assignments	11	4	3	3	2	0	4
Track Room Personalization Program	6	2	2	1	0	1	3
Track Vehicle Usage/ Maintenance/Billing	13	7	14	6	8	2	9
Environmental Control (92 out of 214)							
Monitor/Control Heating/ Cooling Systems	18	40	24	16	2	7	12
Monitor/Control Building Access	8	9	2	1	0	1	2
Monitor/Control Room Access	2	8	3	2	0	0	3
Detect/Report Fires	16	21	11	11	0	3	6
Personnel Management (138 out of 214)							
Maintain Employee Data	41	17	68	40	30	7	23
Record/Summarize Attendance/Leave	23	14	48	22	22	4	14
Prepare Payrolls	10	17	95	31	48	4	17
Evaluate Paraprofessional Staff Applicants	14	6	5	2	4	1	4
Evaluate Paraprofessional Staff Performance	9	5	5	2	4	1	6
Evaluate Other Employees	5	3	4	2	2	1	6
Train Staff (other than in use of computers)	9	0	2	1	0	1	4

TABLE 1 (*continued*)
Housing and Food Service Functions Performed on Computers
(No. Reporting = 214)

Applications	Micro	Mini	Main	O/L	Batch	Prop	New
Other Applications (114 out of 214):							
Assist External Student Affairs Research	27	9	29	15	12	4	14
Route Long-Distance Calls	9	21	27	17	8	7	11
Track/Bill Long-Distance Calls	16	20	54	19	22	6	11
Record/Reconcile/Report Coin-Op Operations	13	1	8	4	4	0	4

KEY TO TABLE 1. *MICRO*—application is run on an independent microcomputer. *MINI OR MAIN*—application is run on a multiterminal departmental minicomputer or a central campus mainframe. *O/L*—Interactive mode usually with immediate output on the screen (for mini and mainframe applications). *BATCH*—input is submitted in batch and output is received later. *PROP* (proprietary)—application uses special purchased software package. *NEW*—application installed since January 1, 1984. Numbers following each section heading indicate how many of the 214 responding institutions reported computer use in one or more applications in that section.

Note: From *Housing and Food Service Functions Performed on Computers* by M. Welch, 1986. Unpublished raw data from survey conducted for the Association of College and University Housing Officers—International. Reprinted by permission.

Not surprisingly, the heaviest use of computers was reported in traditional clerical areas (word processing), large database needs (applications/assignments), and financial calculation (assessment and budgeting). Word processing was concentrated in the local office on microcomputers (**MICRO** column) or other stand-alone equipment, whereas central mainframe computers (**MAIN** column) were heavily favored for recording and processing large volumes of student and financial data and for those activities, such as payrolls, that are applicable campus-wide. Some subject areas, such as conference housing, were divided almost equally between large and small machines, whereas minicomputers (**MINI** column) are being overshadowed and perhaps squeezed out except for certain specialty functions in food services and environmental control. Use of externally purchased application-specific proprietary software (**PROP** column) is very limited, but it is especially interesting to note the large volume of automated processes (**NEW** column) implemented since early 1984.

HARDWARE

Mainframes will usually be selected by a computer services advisory committee composed of representatives from several campus departments. This committee also will have a representative from the purchasing department who will coordinate the request for proposal preparation and the purchasing process. The central computer services department staff will provide the technical expertise, and often chair the advisory committee.

IBM currently provides about 70% of the mainframes in the country, with the balance being provided by Digital Equipment Corporation (DEC), Unisys, Control Data Corporation (CDC), and Honeywell. Mainframes are generally considered to cost in the $700,000 and up category.

In general, it is usually best to select the software and then select the hardware for which that software was designed originally. This is especially true for special stand-alone software applications that operate on minicomputers, but is also true, in general, for all applications. The documentation will usually be better and operation of the software will be easier. The preferred approach in most cases is to buy both the software and hardware as a package system from one vendor who will provide maintenance and support for the entire system, thereby eliminating "finger pointing" when something goes awry. A number of companies manufacture minicomputers. In addition to those in the previous paragraph, minicomputers are manufactured by Hewlett-Packard, Prime, Wang, Altos, Harris, Data General, and others.

Selection of microcomputers is a bit more complicated. All computers utilize a basic software package called an operating system, which differs among microcomputers just as it does among mainframes. Because both the equipment and the software are dependent on the operating system, one must first decide which basic "disk operating system" to use. The first major generic micro operating system was CP/M (Computer Program for Microcomputers) adopted by Apple and several others in the late 1970s. Some vendors, such as Tandy-Radio Shack, developed other proprietary systems. When IBM entered the market in 1981, however, it chose a system developed by Microsoft, which became a de facto standard. Most manufacturers such as Tandy, AT&T, and others have already made at least some if not all of their machines compatible by utilizing this disk operating system, including Apple. Generically, this system is known as MS-DOS (Microsoft Disk Operating System), and IBM's proprietary label is PC-DOS (Personal Computer Disk Operating System). IBM's latest disk operating system, OS/2, released in 1988, may become the standard for the 1990s. It was written to utilize the capabilities of the IBM PS/2 line of microcomputers and will allow multitasking, improved windowing capabilities, and additional random access memory (RAM).

Because thousands of software programs have now been developed for IBM and compatible machines, one would be wise to select micros that can run all that off-the-shelf software. Even within MS-DOS, slight differences may exist between machines. This has given rise to the phrase "IBM-compatible" as a measure of how well a micro can reliably run the many programs developed for PC-DOS.

A typical microcomputer configuration for an office work station should include at least 1MB RAM (random access memory), at least a 60 MB hard disk, a high resolution VGA color monitor, asynchronous communications board, parallel printer board/port, a 5¼" double-sided 360K disk drive and a 1.4MB 3½" disk drive. Because the 3½" disks and disk drives will be the standard by the late 1980s or early 1990s, it would be wise to have both types of drives for total versatility. A less expensive configuration might substitute a monochrome display, but most programs now utilize color so well that one would miss some of the more useful (and colorful) aspects of the newer software. Being able to change colors also eases eyestrain. Most users now purchase the VGA (Video Graphics Array) option and VGA color monitor. Printers are available from many manufacturers. *PC Magazine* reviewed 70 printers that had been introduced from 1984–1985 (Dickinson, 1985) and tested 106 printers and published the results in November 10, 1987 (Howard, 1987). The most popular printers for microcomputer applications have been the dot matrix printers from Epson Corporation. They are very reliable, easy to use, and give one the flexibility of near-letter-quality printing, graphs, and charts. IBM makes a variety of high-quality printers. Others include Xerox (which also owns Diablo), NEC, Okidata, Apple, DEC, Toshiba, and Tandy, to identify a few. Laser printers have become the standard accompaniment for office micros, but are still expensive and have some cumbersome paper handling and envelope printing features. The most popular laser printer is made by Hewlett-Packard. Laser printers produce the best overall print quality and are especially suited for correspondence and other applications requiring the best possible print quality from a micro system. In fact, the print quality from laser printers approaches that of typesetting.

Micros or Minis?

Minicomputers have been on the market for decades and generally are used in applications where a number of users need to be on-line and interactive to a large database. Minicomputers are more expensive than micros, usually selling from $12,000 to $700,000 depending on configuration, memory, and peripherals. Microcomputers are generally desktop units selling for under $12,000 and are used by one individual to do word processing, spreadsheet processing, small database manipulation, and to access mainframes and outside databases. Often microcomputers are networked to share files and communicate with other campus offices. Frequently, a minicomputer, or sometimes a microcomputer with a large capacity hard disk, is utilized as a file server for several microcomputer users. The difference between mini- and microcomputers is becoming less easy to define as technological advances increase and prices continue to drop for micros. It is not uncommon to have a micro with 120 or more megabytes of hard disk storage, which would have clearly been in the minicomputer range a few years ago. Many desktop micros are now more powerful than minis, and even than mainframes of a few decades ago, but they are easier to use and much more flexible. One major trend in the future may be the eventual elimination of the minicomputer, as microcomputers with large hard disk storage capacity begin to dominate the market. As micros continue to drop in price and increase in capability, they become more viable as alternatives for what have previously been solely mainframe and minicomputer applications.

Is the Mainframe Dead?

Absolutely not. Most student affairs offices will continue to use the computer services mainframe on campus for heavy input to and output from the student database, payroll, accounting, scheduling and registration, and other databases, and to run lengthy and complicated jobs. Backup and security are more easily handled on mainframes. A few software vendors can provide program packages for institutional finance or student records that have several modules that can be purchased singly or as a total system. In student records, modules tend to include admissions, academic records, class scheduling, financial aid, accounts receivable, and others. The advantage is that the various modules use similar menus and commands, which makes cross-training easier. They also are integrated, which allows entries in one module common to other modules to easily (and usually automatically) update those other modules.

Because housing and some other student affairs operations do not exist on all campuses and differ a great deal from one campus to another, few vendors have offered generic mainframe software packages for these areas. Existing programs have, therefore, usually been written "in-house" by computer center programmers. Some vendors of institutional student record systems have expressed interest in adding a housing module to their systems and have been looking at housing programs already written on selected campuses to find one or more that could be made generically adaptable.

Mainframes will continue to flourish as the computers of choice for major databases, accounting functions, mass number crunching, and faculty research. They permit sharing of data and transactions among numerous databases, which has significant value in reducing duplicate input effort, providing data on a more timely basis, and eliminating conflicting data. To appreciate this value, one need only think of the number of different offices on campus that record student addresses and have only slow and cumbersome (if any) ways of sharing changes. The rumors of the demise of mainframes are premature and unfounded.

SOFTWARE

There is considerable risk in trying to recommend software packages. Each individual, this author included, has a bias toward certain kinds of hardware and software based on personal experience. Because learning a good comprehensive software package requires from 20 to 80 hours, one is, at times, reluctant to try new products. New products and updates of current products are continually being introduced, making it difficult to report them in a book and be current. To remain current regarding software one needs to review magazines and periodicals, such as *PC Magazine* and *PcWeek*. Acknowledging these biases, and the fact that this information will quickly be out of date, the following observations regarding current software are offered.

Spreadsheet Software

Spreadsheet programs are the easiest software packages to learn to use. There are also fewer packages available to confuse the potential buyer. Basically a spreadsheet program creates a numerical table, such as the typical financial statement, in which any entry or cell may contain original data, a formula dependent on one or more cells of original data, or permanent labels. Each time any original data cell is changed, all dependent formula cells are automatically recalculated. This capability not only saves calculation time and errors but also allows quick determination of possible alternatives, such as the financial impact of an increase in room rates or a decline in occupancy or enrollment. Furthermore, sections of the spreadsheet can be moved or copied at will while the program automatically adjusts formulas to reflect the new locations of dependent data.

Supercalc, Lotus 1-2-3, Quattro, Excel, and Multiplan are, clearly, the current favorites users across the country. Lotus 1-2-3 is now the best-seller, but some object to its annoying copy protection routines, which Lotus has promised to eliminate in its release announced for late 1989.

Visicalc, introduced in 1977, was the original spreadsheet software, and probably did more to legitimize microcomputers than any other software introduction. Visicalc was followed by Multiplan and then Supercalc, which was introduced in 1980. Lotus 1-2-3 was introduced in early 1983 with an aggressive marketing campaign. Symphony, an integrated Lotus 1-2-3 spreadsheet with word processing and database management, was introduced in the mid-1980s, but its some 500 or so commands resulted in less-than-favorable market response, except for those whose primary job function was complicated financial analysis. It also uses an extensive amount of memory. Supercalc is now in its sixth update and the parent company, Sorcim, was purchased by Computer Associates, a larger firm with better marketing capability. Supercalc is a popular spreadsheet package is very attractive to users because of its ease of use and the fact that it it not copy protected. It also offers a database capability and excellent 3D graphics. Microsoft Excel has experienced strong sales and features excellent presentation quality and graphics in a windows environment. Several other spreadsheet programs are available, but have limited users.

Database Software

The choices get a bit more complicated for database packages, but the clear favorite is dBASE, followed by R Base, Powerbase, KnowledgeMan, Condor, Revelation, PCFile, Pfs:File, and a host of others. A new database program offered by Borland called Paradox has been well received by users.

Database programs generally fall into two categories: "flat-file managers" or "relational databases." All deal with items of informtion (such as room assignments or parents' name) for each of a group of entities (such as individual students). Each piece of data is a field, each group of fields about an entity is a record, and each set of records is a file. File manager programs provide varied and sometimes complex methods of organizing the file, entering data, answering specific queries, and printing reports. Relational database programs provide similar capabilities but also tie multiple files together to permit entering data to two or more different files from the same screen, to update other files when data are changed in one, and to report data from multiple files on the same screen or printout. Many relational database programs go yet a step further to offer their own programming languages, which permit more complex, specialized, and useful reports and inter-file relationships, but which require considerably more effort to learn. *PC Magazine* offered a comprehensive review of 26 flat-file managers, 24 relational databases, and 32 programmable relational databases in two summer issues of 1986 (Krosnoff, June 24, 1986; July, 1986). Additional reviews were made in 1988 (Seymour, 1988) and 1989 (Shaw, 1989). The various computer magazines periodically update their reviews of software.

dBASE by the Ashton Tate Company was the first really popular database management program. Even though the original documentation was poor and difficult to understand, hundreds of thousands of the software packages were sold, and a wealth of experience exists nationwide regarding dBASE, which makes it easy to swap files and programming routines with other campuses. dBASE has been updated several times, and the current release is titled dBASE IV. Ashton Tate also markets an integrated database, spreadsheet, and word processing package called Framework. Again, the difficulty in learning all the commands and functions of an integrated package has resulted in slow acceptance of Framework.

Fourth-generation programming languages should result in database programs being more user-friendly, with increased use of English language commands to manipulate the data. For now, though, one is probably wise to stick with the most popular database programs to benefit from the large user base and applications.

Word Processing Software

Many word processing packages are available, all of which require a commitment of time to learn. They are the current version of automated general writing aids that have progressed through manual, electric, electronic, and memory typewriters and more sophisticated individual and network-dedicated word processing systems. In fact, IBM's microcomputer version of Displaywrite was adapted directly from its Displaywriter series of word processing machines, and Multimate's Advantage was purposely designed to emulate similar Wang word processors.

Far beyond simple typing, such packages permit numerous variations of formats and type styles within a single page or document, automatically hyphenate and paginate, check spelling, suggest synonyms, produce outlines, assign and print page and footnote numbers, appropriately position and format footnotes, permit insertion of graphs or tables created by other programs, and retrieve data such as addresses from files to insert in form letters. The January 28, 1986, issue (Dickinson, 1986) and February 29, 1988, issue (Seymour, 1988) of *PC Magazine* include excellent reviews of word processing programs. The Editors'

Choice was WordPerfect and they offered the following statement: "The present market leader in word processing programs. Easy import of files created in other leading programs—plus mail-merge, outlining, redlining, table of authorities, and desktop publishing interface—makes it a corporate power to be reckoned with. Not copy protected." Wordstar was one of the earliest word processing packages for microcomputers in a variety of disk operating system versions. It has been updated several times, with the last update being release 5.5 in 1989.

More microcomputers are used for word processing than any other function (see Table 1). Because Wordstar was one of the first word processing packages, it has one of the largest user groups of any software package in existence today.

Other popular word processing packages are Multimate, PFS:Write, Microsoft Word, IBM Displaywrite, Wordstar 2000, Volkswriter Deluxe, MacWrite, Applewrite, and a host of others. WordPerfect 5.0 is the leading word processing package for the late 1980s and early 1990s and features a built-in spelling checker, thesaurus, and a number of other helpful features. It also incorporates some desktop publishing features and diverse font capability. Microsoft Word, Multimate, and IBM's Displaywrite also are used heavily on campuses.

The decision regarding a word processing package depends on the support for training that is available on campus. Because word processing is used to handle the clerical functions in an office and the turnover rate can be high for clerical positions, it is wise to make sure there is some standardization on campus, at leat in the student affairs division, to make training of new staff easier. Standardization also allows electronic transfer of documents from one office to another, eases problem solving and support services, and allows easy adaptation when staff transfer from one office to another. One of the few disadvantages of computerization is that it is more difficult to train new staff. It is more complicated than simply bringing in a new person to operate a typewriter. Office efficiency and continuity depend on choosing a software package that has the most widespread campus use and training support.

Desktop Publishing Software

One of the most significant and exciting trends in the mid to late 1980s was the advent of desktop publishing. Desktop publishing is a phrase coined in part to describe WYSIWYG (what you see is what you get), which displays exactly on the screen what the printed page will look like. Desktop publishing is page-oriented and allows the user to incorporate graphs, pictures, or cartoons to create a professional looking document of near-typeset quality. Desktop publishing is most useful for newsletters, flyers, announcements, and a host of short documents. It is not intended to replace word processing for producing daily correspondence, or long manuscripts and book chapters such as this one simply because the time spent formatting the page and selecting type fonts for each page would be too cumbersome. It is likely that new updates of present word processing packages will continue to incorporate more desktop publishing functions and that present desktop publishing software will incorporate more sophisticated word processing functions. The more a professional image is sought for presentation materials the more likely one is to use desktop publishing over word processing. There also is much development taking place in merging desktop publishing software with typesetting to deliver quality products.

Currently the most popular desktop publishing software is available from Aldus, a Seattle, Washington, firm; it was operated originally only on the Apple Macintosh computer. The program was released in late 1986 for IBM microcomputers. Because desktop publishing technology is undergoing rapid development and change, microcomputer users will want to follow their favorite weekly or monthly publication to remain current regarding trends.

Other General Microcomputer Software

Beyond the three major microcomputer areas of word processing, spreadsheets, and databases are several other useful types of programs. First among these are the "integrated" packages that usually combine spreadsheets, database management, word processing, communications, graphics, and other utlities in a single software package. They utilize common menus and commands, which promote reduced training time and more efficient use by people who need more than one application. Further "integration" results from built-in routines that transfer data from one function to another, such as putting data from a file into a spreadsheet and calculating further data that are then set up in a table or graph and inserted between paragraphs in a report.

At this writing, the most popular integrated packages are Symphony by Lotus, Framework by Ashton-Tate, and Enable by the Software Group, which were reviewd on June 10, 1986 (Poor, 1986) by *PC Magazine*. Several others are available. Typically, the trade-off for ease of use has been loss of the advanced features and flexibility of individual stand-alone programs. In addition, it is more difficult to learn three or more major software functions at one time as opposed to learning one package, such as word processing, before going on to another package. Integrated packages have been significantly improved, and may be quite suitable for many users.

Another way of making varied programs more compatible without giving up power, particularly for people who need to switch regularly from one function to another throughout the day, is to utilize a "window" program. Present competitors are IBM's Topview, Microsoft Windows, GEM Desktop, and DESQview. Although they have limitations and have experienced a varied reception in the market, these or similar improved programs may well develop a loyal following.

Other significant functional programs include "graphics" programs that can provide a myriad pictorial representations of data to enhance their comprehension and impact, and "communications" programs that facilitate access and transfer of data between computers of the same or very dissimilar sizes and types whether across the room, the campus, or the country.

"Screen formatters" permit the user to "paint" the computer screen with a variety of formats, colors, boxes, and other symbols to make on-screen forms used in many types of programs more readable, less eye-straining, and, therefore, more useful and less prone to input errors. "Desk organizers" can interrupt other programs to provide instant access to an on-screen calculator, the user's appointment calendar (with a reminder alarm clock), a notepad, and a phone list that can even dial the phone. "Key programmers" increase user speed by attaching almost any series of repetitive or often-used commands to a single key or combination of keys so that the user need only press the simple combination to execute the entire set of commands. Other utilities are also available to organize files on large-capacity disks, to provide back-up copies of files, to help utilize all the capabilities of printers, and to insulate the user from memorizing cryptic commands by creating screen menus. There are even utilities to recover files erased in error.

Food Service Systems

Two primary types of systems are available for university food service operations. One is an overall food production management system and the other controls access or accounts receivable and cash management. Several companies specialize in one or the other of these systems, but no company has yet emerged as a leader in offering both systems.

C-BORD's Menu Management System and Griffin's Vali-Dine access and debit card system are the most popular and best established among university food service users. A food service management system helps manage food production, inventory, forecasting, precosting, warehousing and purchasing, postcost, vendor purchasing history, and a number of other functions. A variety of management reports are available. The C-BORD Menu Management System was originally known as the "Sentry" system and was developed at Cornell University. This system previously ran on mainframes and minis and now runs on the IBM-AT, PS/2, or IBM-compatible machines. C-BORD also provides capability to network PCs in various food units on a campus.

Another overall food management system is available from Concept Systems. The people who developed this system previously worked for ARA Food Services; therefore, the system has similarities to the ARA "Focus" system.

Griffin Technology, Inc., is the developer of the popular Vali-Dine dining room entry system. Griffin leases its products only as a total system package. It utilizes a nonstandard magnetic stripe on its ID card, but can also provide an ABA stripe similar to major credit cards. Its access system offers a variety of configurations for standard mandatory board plans, debit a-la-carte service, credit a-la-carte, and a variety of combinations in between these types of services. Griffin Technology manufactures its own minicomputer and writes its own software.

Harco Industries is relatively new to the university ID card access system business, but has had considerable experience in the industrial security access field and reports from three of their users—Duke, Indiana, and Penn State—indicate that Harco's transition to the university climate has been good. The system design is comparable to Griffin, but runs on a DEC minicomputer. You can purchase the system. Harco's ID card uses an ABA Track II standard magnetic stripe. Identicard Systems, Inc., also offers an access system.

A campus is well served if it can combine the dining access system card with an all-campus ID card. This allows students the convenience of carrying only one card. With careful planning, the system can be used for library access, recreation facility access, dining access, residence hall access, grocery store charges, bookstore charges, test center access, check cashing, and virtually any other campus service that requires authorized access or clearance, or needs a tie-in to accounts receivable or a declining "debit" system.

Computerized Reservations Systems

These systems are designed to handle the day-to-day nonacademic scheduling needs of a college or university. Although they are designed primarily for a union building operation, they may be adapted to many other scheduling situations as well. The two best known systems are the

Welber Micro-Computer College-Union Scheduling-System and Room and Event Scheduling Software (RESS) offered by Philip J. Niehoff and marketed through Integrated Management Systems Ltd. Users report excellent experience with both systems.

Vending Machine Management Systems

Most universities use an off-the-shelf database or spreadsheet software package to manage their soft drink, washer-dryer, candy-snack, and other vending operations. Two companies offer vending machine management systems: Effective Management Systems, Milwaukee, WI; and Data Intelligence Systems Corporation, Cambridge, MA. Both systems run on a DEC minicomputer and perform the same basic tasks.

Time Management Systems

Several companies are developing time management systems that utilize an employee ID card in place of a time card. The systems should be designed to calculate hours worked, premium pay, pay due, a scheduled hours versus actual hours worked comparison, exception report printouts, labor cost to sales comparison, and customers served as compared with labor hours. This system should be a standard system for the entire campus to facilitate electronic transfer to the central payroll office. Harco, C-BORD, and Griffin are all developing these types of systems, or interfaces to other systems already on the market, for the university market. Others include the KRONOS and Matrix Systems.

Housekeeping and Maintenance Systems

Itek Engineering, in Atlanta, seems to have the largest following among housing and physical plant administrators. It offers microcomputer software for housekeeping, work order, and maintenance functions. It also provides building maintenance, systems, and energy conservation surveys. Hewlett-Packard also has a system that has received favorable reviews but is limited to use on that company's computers.

Housing Management Systems

There is no widely used standard software package currently being marketed for housing assignments, related statistics, and waiting lists. One company, Applied Collegiate Systems in Irving, Texas, has marketed housing information systems for colleges and universities since 1983. Most universities interface their housing assignments with the central student database, and most of these systems have usually been written by campus programmers for use on the central campus mainframes. A number of campuses have developed excellent housing, food service, housekeeping, and maintenance systems; however, none of these campus-developed systems to date have been marketed for widespread use by other universities. Reportedly Western Kentucky University is considering nationwide marketing of its housing system.

Student Database and Accounting Systems

Information Associates seems to have the most popular software for university accounting and also provides a student database system. Its software runs on both mainframes and minis and can be acquired in modules. It also offers a financial aids management package. Information Associates has merged with Management Science America (MSA) in Atlanta but will be operated as a wholly owned subsidiary.

Other firms that offer financial accounting systems and modules to serve various other functions are McCormack & Dodge, Cullinet, Data Design Associates, Software International, and American Management Systems. Probably the most important consideration in selecting a student database package is to find a software package that most closely matches the needs of the institution, modify it as little as possible or not at all, and run it on the hardware for which it was written. In future years, the major cost of management information systems will be for software as hardware costs continue to decline.

Where Do You Buy Software?

Microcomputer software can be obtained inexpensively from mail-order houses at prices often slightly above half other vendors' list price. The two best known are PC Connection and 47th Street Computer. Both carry multipage ads in popular microcomputer magazines. Those who have used these two mail-order companies report good service and prompt delivery, but caution that neither company is equipped to deal with university purchase order and billing procedures. A check with each order or utilization of a charge card is recommended when ordering from either company. Other than answering simple questions by phone, the company provides no software support. Local computer stores provide more support, but also charge more for the software. One service, Chambers and Associates, obtains special arrangements and prices from software companies for sales to higher education. The prices are discounted as much as 80% off the normal retail price. The software, however, is restricted to classroom and other educational uses. Campus computer centers are also often able to obtain special pricing through educational discounts, site licenses, and other techniques.

NETWORKING

About 80% of microcomputer networking communication occurs within a single building. As a result, local area networks (LANs) may make sense for electronic mail and transfer of documents. The least expensive method of communication is the simple transfer of a floppy disk or other electronic media. It is also the least complicated and most reliable. The most sophisticated networks are those that serve an entire campus. These systems consist of a series of minicomputers with PCs and terminals with the minis tied to mainframes. These systems allow on-line interactive communication with virtually any terminal or PC on campus and also may feature access by residence hall students from their room with the library or other campus databases with which they are authorized to communicate. There are any number of possible configurations and possibilities. Although several schemes for networking microcomputers have been introduced, there is much room for improvement. No standards have yet emerged, thus it would be wise to exercise extra caution in selecting and implementing a LAN. There are, though, a number of reliable national networks available via phone modem for everything from shopping to simple sharing of information.

TRAINING

People are the most important factor to consider when computerizing. Computers do not replace people—they simply allow people to be more creative and productive. Computers also make work more enjoyable by reducing the redundant and repetitive tasks involved. It is natural, however, for people to feel insecure and intimidated by the new technology. How you deal with these feelings will determine the success of your computerization process.

Consider buying portable computers that your staff can take home for several weeks. Hide the complicated and intimidating manuals; provide only the fundamental information in a three-ring binder, along with the software disks. Let someone who has learned the system recently serve as the trainer and resource person for the rest of your staff. This person, who has recently made all the mistakes of a beginner, will likely be a patient teacher and friend who remembers all too well the pitfalls and frustrations of getting started.

Allowing people to work at their own pace, in their chosen environment, without getting entangled in all the computer jargon, will produce amazing results. Both employees and employers have to make time available for this learning process in an atmosphere that is enjoyable. The simple fact that your organization cares enough to provide training will improve job satisfaction and morale. People will become more excited about their jobs. They, as well as you, will become more creative in finding easier and better ways to handle the routine and repetitive tasks involved in providing services to students. Those services, as well as employee morale, will improve. Your staff also will overcome their fear of computers.

This type of training is now under way on several campuses across the country, as well as in business and industry. Some firms use information centers; many campuses have user groups that meet periodically to discuss software, hardware, and their own frustrations and successes. These computer training ideas are the most positive people management trends that have been observed recently on several campuses. They show employees that administrators do care about their growth and development.

GETTING STARTED

Many university administrators have been progressive in computerizing a multitude of campus functions. As the cost of computers declines, software continues to improve, and both software and hardware become easier to use, more administrators will desire computerization. Many management systems previously available only for a minicomputer or mainframe are now available for microcomputers at one third the cost or even less, and are much easier to use.

This manager's real plunge into computerization occurred when IBM introduced its PC in 1981. A campus decision was made to standardize microcomputing using that machine, prompting the housing staff to install computer labs in the residence halls. An extra machine was purchased to serve as a ready source of spare parts. The best site found to store the machine, fortunately, was in this administrator's office. Behind closed doors and on weekends the learning process began that eventually spread to most of the staff. A training program was developed; about 60 staff members, including the president and two vice presidents, took the training materials and a computer home.

The excitement and creativity that was unleashed was simply incredible. One early participant won a US Steel-NACUBO cost-saving award for an application he developed to cost wage and benefit packages during labor negotiations. Every participant developed creative, job-specific applications.

How is the cost of the program justified? In the 1960s no one hesitated to buy a $1,500 mechanical calculator for administrative staff. In today's dollars those calculators cost more than current microcomputers. Why should we hesitate? If we place computer labs in residence halls, there is a significant convenience and safety benefit; students no longer need to trek across campus to the central computer center or an academic lab. Typing labs have been common in residence halls—the computer is today's typewriter. Student affairs staff working with students will identify a multitude of potential applications that will improve services for students and make it more attractive for them to live on campus. Employees will find new and exciting ways to accomplish many of the repetitive and boring tasks associated with their jobs.

As a student affairs professional, how should you begin with computerization? Start with a spreadsheet package like Supercalc or Lotus 1-2-3. They are easy to use, especially if you begin with your budget. This administrator has responsibility for large budgets in many different accounts. Manually, it took over 30 hours to update changes during the budget and rate proposal process. After putting these budgets on Supercalc spreadsheets, an update could be made in 15 minutes to 2 hours. Illustrative graphs could be generated to simplify explanations of the budgets to the vice presidents, president, and board of trustees.

The increased level of confidence inspired by the ease with which one could manipulate the data led to a reduction in room and board rates for 1 year, an almost unheard of occurrence on a university campus. From a beginning like this, you will find many relatively easy applications, such as word processing, damage billings, general ledgers, a variety of financial reports, mailing lists, preventive maintenance schedules, work schedules, rosters, name tags, newsletters, library access and advising, to name just a few. Some more complicated applications, like conference management, waiting lists, networking, and electronic mail will naturally follow. You will also want to consider systems that can be purchased for food service management, housekeeping, maintenance, financial aid management, union building scheduling, and so on. They are relatively easy to use, have a quick payback, and significantly improve services for students.

THE FUTURE

In 35 years, we have gone from computers that took up entire rooms with immense air conditioning systems, to today's desktop computers boasting equal or greater power. There is little reason to believe that we will not experience similar progress in the next 30 or so years. Microcomputers have been available only since 1975, with significant sales occurring only since 1981.

In late 1985, Portia Isaacson, the founder of Future Computing, made a speech in Nashville at the Information Center Conference and Exhibition, a meeting attended by computer experts from around the world. In her remarks, she gave her view of the future:

> Half of all office workers will have access to a personal computer by the end of 1985 and 19% will have one on their desk. Within five years, 70% of them will have personal computers on their desks, 25% will have more than one, and by 1995, they will be required on nearly every desk.
>
> IBM obviously dominates the industry, and other manufacturers will not last much longer if their products are not IBM-compatible, or capable of using the same software developed for IBM's products. The issue of compatibility with IBM is extremely important to all of us. Thank goodness they are American.
>
> Advances in both the hardware and software will continue but the major breakthroughs will be in computer software. Still, by 1990, $6,000 will buy a microcomputer with 19 million bytes of random access memory, 100 million bytes of hard disk storage, 1 billion bytes of storage on an optical disk, a laser printer, and a 4,800 baud modem. (Gregory, 1985)

Ms. Isaacson's predictions made in 1985 have occurred even sooner than she predicted. There are, indeed, countless other breakthroughs occurring in the world of computers such as fourth-generation languages, artificial intelligence (expert systems), and even intelligent computers (IBM's Intellect was an early version). Reports generated by voice-actuated English-language commands soon will be commonplace. Most library books eventually will be on optical disks tied to computers and high-speed laser printers. Students will be able to print out an entire book, or whatever part of it they need, paying a small fee for the service and copyright permission.

From their residence hall rooms, students on all campuses will have access to the campus computer center, libraries, external databases, and shopping services. Forms and brochures will be typed on the office word processor, transmitted electronically to the campus printing services computerized typesetter and, for some jobs, sent directly to the high-speed laser printer. Printing services will not have to rekey the document. Spelling and typing errors will be all but eliminated.

Desktop publishing already has come of age and is leading to exciting improvements in the quality of newsletters, announcements, and forms. Page scanning equipment will eliminate the necessity to rekey documents. Disk backup equipment will improve as a result of more offices using larger hard disk drives. CD-ROM (compact laser disks for large volume storage) technology will mature, and the prospect of having large reference files available for access by the PCs across campus is exciting.

Small laptop microcomputers now are as powerful as desktop models of only a few years ago. Pocket and notebook models with the power of current desktops are on the way. Notebook-size computers that recognize handwriting and eliminate the keyboard are also on the way. The readability of display screens on portables and laptops will improve dramatically.

Microcomputer chip technology will continue to improve. The 80386SX chip will likely become the entry-level standard with 80386 full 32-bit capability micros becoming the office standard. The 80486 chip will probably become the standard in the 1990s.

Consider again the elimination of redundant and boring tasks in our electronic age. This is the most exciting era yet for university administrators. If you, as a student affairs administrator, are not yet involved with computers, make this the year to be so. If you are involved already, plow ahead. The rewards for you, your staff, and the students will be immeasurable.

REFERENCES

Dickinson, J. (1985, September 17). Printers. *PC Magazine*, pp. 92–193.

Dickinson, J. (1986, January 28). The business of words—corporate, professional, personal. *PC Magazine*, pp. 93–251.

Gregory, E. (1985, August 21). Desk-top computer use foreseen. *The Tennessean*, pp. 1–D, 4–D.

Howard, B. (1987, November 10). The 4th annual all-printer review. *PC Magazine,* pp. 92–420.

Krosnoff, B. (1986, June 24). Flat file databases. *PC Magazine*, pp. 187–249.

Krosnoff, B., & Dickinson, J. (1986, July). *Project Database*, pp. 106–252.

Poor, A. (1986, June 10). Integration with integrity: Framework, Symphony, and Enable. *PC Magazine*, pp. 127–151.

Seymour, J. (1988, February 29). Fast, flexible, & forward-looking. *PC Magazine*, pp. 92–344.

Seymour, J. (1988, May 17). Project Database 3, programmable databases: dBase and its challengers. *PC Magazine*, pp. 93–304.

Shaw, R.H. (1989, June 13). Databases for OS/2: The first wave. *PC Magazine*, pp. 94–122.

Welch, M. (1986). *Housing and food service functions performed on computers.* Unpublished raw data from survey conducted for the Association of College and University Housing Officers—International.

COMPANY AND MAGAZINE ADDRESSES

Aldus Corporation, Suite 200, 411 First Avenue South, Dept. D., Seattle, WA 98104. (206) 622-5500. Page Maker software for desktop publishing.

Applied Collegiate Systems, 500 MacArthur Commons, 3501 N. MacArthur Blvd., Irving, TX 75062. (800) 426-8936. Housing informations systems.

C-Bord Inc., Suite 300, First Bank Building, The Commons, Ithaca, NY 14850. (607) 272-2410. Menu Management, access control, and a variety of other food service software.

Chambers and Associates, 5499 N. Federal Highway, Boca Raton, FL 33431. (305) 997-9444. Provides microcomputer software to education community at up to 80% discounts.

Concept Systems Inc., One Franklin Plaza, Suite 650, Philadelphia, PA 19102. (215) 563-1425. Food service production and related software.

Cullinet, 400 Blue Hill Drive, Westwood, MA 02090. (617) 329-7700. Integrated financial informtion systems.

Data Design Associates, 1279 Oakmead Parkway, Sunnyvale, CA 94086. (408) 730-0100. Integrated financial information systems.

Data Intelligence Systems Corporation, 19 Monsignor O'Brien Highway, Cambridge, MA 02141. (617) 227-5405. Vending machine management software.

Effective Management Systems, Inc., 1701 West Civic Drive, Milwaukee, WI 53209. (800) 588-8727. Vending machine management software.

Griffin Technology Inc., 6132 Victor Manchester Road, Victor, NY 14564. (716) 924-7121. Vali-Dine access system and other related food service software.

Harco Industries, Inc., 10802 North 21st Avenue, Phoenix, AZ (602) 944-1565. Dining room access system.

Identicard Systems Inc., 630 East Oregon Road, Box 5349, Lancaster, PA 17601 (717) 569-5756. Dining room access system.

Information Associates, Inc., 1150 Sunset Hills Rd., Suite 200, Reston, VA 22090. (703) 478-9350. Integrated student database and financial information systems.

Integrated Management Systems Ltd., 2301 Harley Drive, Madison, WI 53711. (608) 274-9479. Room and event scheduling software.

Itex Corporation, 2704 Highway 120, Suite B, Duluth, GA 30136. (404) 476-1944. Software and consulting services for physical plant operations.

Kronos Inc., 62 Fourth Avenue, Waltham, MA 02154. (800) 225-1561. Microcomputer time clock accounting systems.

MacUser, Subscription Dept., 29 Haviland Street, S. Norwalk, CT 06854. (203) 853-1858. Monthly publication for Apple Macintosh users.

Management Science America (MSA), Inc., 3445 Peachtree Rd., Atlanta, GA 30326-1276. (404) 239-2000. Business financial software.

Matrix Systems, Inc., 1948 West Dorothy Lane, Dayton, OH 45439. (513) 293-9333. Time clock management software.

McCormack & Dodge, 1225 Worcester Road, Natick, MA. (617) 655-8200. Integrated financial information systems.

PC Connection, 6 Mill Street, Marlow, NH 03456. (603) 446-3383 or (800) 243-8088. Mail-order source of software and hardware at substantial discounts from retail prices.

PC Magazine, P.O. Box 2445, Boulder, CO 80322. (303) 447-9330. Independent guide to IBM and IBM compatible microcomputer users.

PC Week Magazine, Circulation Dept., One Park Avenue, 4th Floor, New York, NY 10016. (212) 503-5408. Independent journal published weekly for IBM and IBM compatible users.

Publish, Subscription Dept., P.O. Box 51966, Boulder, CO 80321-1966. (800) 525-0643. The how-to magazine of desktop publishing.

47th Street Computer, 36 East 19th Street, New York, NY 10003. (212) 260-4410 or (800) 221-7774. Mail-order source of software and hardware at substantial discounts from retail prices.

Elliu R. Welber, 634 30th St., San Francisco, CA 94131. (415) 648-1107. Computerized reservations and event scheduling system.

CHAPTER 4

Dimensions of Financial Management in Admissions Services

Linda M. Clement

Many student affairs staff and most chief student affairs officers are drawn into overall financial management issues that institutions of higher education face. Terms that were somewhat foreign to the profession a decade ago, such as *enrollment management* and *institutional marketing*, have become "household words" in discussions of the financial management of higher education. At the heart of discussions of financial management are questions related to enrollment and the role of admissions operations in securing the number and types of students specified in institutional goals. If student affairs professionals are to participate fully in the institutional planning process, they should understand the meaning of enrollment management and its impact on tuition, fees, and demand for services. Also, it is crucial that student affairs professionals understand funding of enrollment-related services, and appreciate some of the current issues institutions are facing in the area of admissions. Admissions offices deal with two different types of financial management dimensions—the impact of enrollment on institutional revenues, and the management of office operational expenses. This chapter addresses selected issues in both realms.

THE IMPACT OF ENROLLMENT ON INSTITUTIONAL REVENUES

Enrollment Management

As colleges and universities consider their future, there is a growing concern related to the maintenance of enrollment. Two primary factors contribute to this concern:

1. Undergraduate enrollment is conservatively expected to decline by as much as 30% nationally by 1997. This conclusion is based upon consideration of demographic trends, analysis of the projected ages and racial mix of students, and reasonable projections regarding retention trends of students (Carnegie Council, 1980).
2. College operating costs are increasing at rates more rapid than the revenues generated from tuition and fund-raising (Kotler & Fox, 1985).

Both of these factors threaten the future of institutions of higher education. Certainly declines will not be proportional across all institutions of higher education. Five types of institutions seem most vulnerable: (1) small liberal arts colleges with low name recognition, (2) private, single-sex, 2-year institutions, (3) small newly created private institutions designed to serve very specific clients, (4) middle-level, private urban universities, and (5) remote state colleges located in regions experiencing sharp population declines. The colleges in these categories are more likely to be affected by demographic shifts, rising operating costs, and insecure and small endowments (Mayhew, 1979). It should also be noted that many other types of institutions that are not facing enrollment declines, such as state universities (Ludwig & Stockton, 1987), are finding it difficult to enroll the types of students—talented, minorities, and specific majors—that they seek.

Colleges and universities concerned about their future are engaging in the process of *enrollment management*. This process entails an institution's examining its mission, goals, objectives, and operating procedures and refining them in order to maximize its operation. In its best form, this process involves a wide range of people, with broad input from internal and external constituents. Desired results of the process include: the formulation of a shared understanding of the institution's distinctive educational mission, realistic plans for the recruitment of the student population that can best be served, and concrete plans for retention of students. The process would result in the development of plans that vigorously evaluate enrollment efforts and channel this information back into the systems in order to facilitate institutional planning (Kotler, 1986).

Marketing, recruiting, admissions, and financial aid are certainly most directly involved in the process of enrollment management, but there are also significant links to and influences on orientation, academic advising, institutional research, and retention efforts (Hossler, 1984). The process of enrollment management may find its impetus in the admissions services arena, but it is a process that must have broad-based institutional support if various components are to work in harmony to effectively manage enrollment.

Impact of Enrollment Management on Tuition and Fees and the Relationship Between Enrollment Demands and Services

All institutions of higher education are dependent upon enrollment to generate income. Private institutions rely heavily on tuition revenues. One landmark study (Jenny & Wynn, 1972) that supports this idea notes that in 48 small colleges, income from tuition and fees provided for all instructional costs and operating costs. State-supported institutions are dependent upon tuition itself, and the overwhelming majority are dependent upon enrollment-based appropriations as well. Hence, enrollment management issues related to tuition and fees are vital to the operation of an institution.

In managing enrollment, various elements can be manipulated, depending upon the institution's missions, goals, and needs. The "class mix" is a term utilized to describe the various subpopulations that compose an entering class. Varying the percentages of out-of-state and in-state students, freshman and transfer students, full-time and part-time students, and paying and aid-dependent students each affects the tuition resources, weighted credit hour ratios, demand for financial aid, and income from fees. The class mix in terms of academic talent can dictate demand for particular programs and services such as honors programs, study skills, and tutorial support. Varying the class mix in terms of age, race, geographic distribution, and physical disabilities (physical and learning) can also affect the demand for student services such as housing, counseling, academic support, and transportation. Typically the driving force shaping the class mix is the generation of tuition revenues and adherence to policy dictates of governing boards. The astute student affairs professional must understand the parameters of the class mix and realize that enrollment managment decisions affect the demand for and design of services to students.

Although the management of enrollment, and in particular the class mix, affects the demand for services, the provision of services can affect an institution's potential enrollment. For example, a student's decision to enroll at a particular institution may be influenced by the availability of housing, the positive impact of an orientation program, or the availability of particular intramural sports or other social/recreational activities (Keller & McKeowan, 1984). Optimally, the symbiotic relationship between enrollment management and provision of student services is recognized by university officials involved in these processes.

Decisions regarding enrollment management also heavily affect the generation of particular student fees. Orientation, registration, parking, student activities, health fees, and others are definitely affected by the types of students, particularly when these fees are based on such variables as class level, residency, or part-time/full-time enrollment status. For example, in some insitutions allocation of fees is based upon FTE (full-time equivalency) rather than head count, so decisions to enroll more part-time students affect demand for services.

How enrollment is managed influences many aspects of an institution. Tuition revenues, appropriations based upon enrollment, and fees are most obviously correlated with enrollment. There are also financial implications for services related to student characteristics that are defined in the process of enrollment management.

Funding of Admissions Offices

Of primary importance in maintaining an adequate undergraduate enrollment is the provision of adequate funding for recruitment and admissions programs. It is important that the operation be sufficiently funded, that the source of this funding be dependable and secure, and that in special circumstances additional funding sources be available.

As a general rule, institutions should have one full-time professional admissions officer for each 100–150 new FTE enrollment in an entering class. This would include a cost for both salaries and operating expenses of approximately 10% of gross FTE tuition (Mayhew, 1979). These estimates are, of course, dependent upon how critical the enrollment issue is for a particular college. Institutions must balance issues of cost with the balance they ascribe to overall enrollment goals as well as class mix goals.

Unfortunately, few admissions offices are adequately funded, resulting in inadequate staff and operation expenses and often a patchwork of arrangements that can be inefficient and ineffective. This results in admissions offices not developing the requisite skills and techniques necessary to manage effectively (Ihlanfeldt, 1980). Examples of this in the area of staffing include: hiring admissions officers as contract employees rather than as full-time professional staff, and hiring staff on "match" or temporary lines that must be renewed yearly. Such practices result in high turnover and work against attracting the most talented people. Examples in the operating area include: having postage responsibilities (methods and budget) located in another unit outside of admissions, and having decisions regarding the volume and quality of recruitment literature made by another unit. These examples highlight the need for the routine admissions budget to be adequate to meet demands, and the need for decisions relating to that budget and attendant activities to be controlled by the admissions staff.

Another aspect of admissions funding that merits review is the use of application fees. Admissions offices do not generally receive additional revenues from the generation of application fees that exceed the expected budget. Hence, an admissions office that successfully generates additional applications faces the prospect of processing those applications with the same resources budgeted to process fewer applications. A more flexible system for reversions of application fees should be considered as a justifiable way to address this concern.

The funding issues for admissions offices generally relate to maintenance of an adequate funding level when demands in this area have increased disproportionately in comparison to budget increases. If admissions offices are going to be efficient and effective, institutions will need to examine these issues.

CURRENT ISSUES

Marketing Strategy as an Institutional Tool—Can We Afford to Ignore This Movement?

The financial issues related to admissions and enrollment management are broad and varied. They include considerations related to institutional planning as well as those related to internal office management. A discussion of some of these key issues follows.

The use of marketing principles in the nonprofit sector is a notion that has gained considerable acceptance in higher education circles. At its core, marketing assists institutions to see themselves from the consumer's (student's) point of view. A solid marketing plan does not involve "selling"—the common stereotypical image—but does include extensive self-study. Marketing plans take into account an institution's history and its aspirations, and also its fiscal, political, educational, and philosophical structures (Topor, 1983). Marketing is a process or a methodology that enables institutional leaders to think systematically about the organizational mission, the services, and the market served, and to consider potential new markets (Ihlanfeldt, 1980).

Developing a marketing plan involves a broad cross-section of people on a college campus. Broad-based involvement both ensures the accuracy of the outcome and elicits a commitment for what will be necessary in the implementation of a marketing plan. It will involve serious consideration of the four P's that have become known as the "marketing mix":

- Product (Does the institution need to adapt or change curriculum, services, etc.?)
- Place (Does the institution make the best possible use of its location?)
- Price (Is adjustment of the price necessary, feasible, or admissible?)
- Promote (How can the institution reach targeted audiences in a compelling way)? (Topor, 1983; Smith & Hunt, 1986)

Through an understanding of the above, the successful marketing plan analyzes the environment, potential markets, and competition; analyzes strengths and weaknesses; develops a clear sense of the institution's mission; targets markets; and positions an institution to compete (Kotler & Fox, 1985).

Although the terminology of marketing has found its way into the modern educator's vocabulary, it is still rare to find institutions that wholeheartedly embrace a marketing philosophy. Institutions that could serve as examples in this regard include: Goucher College, the University of Southern California, Northwestern University, and the University of Pennsylvania. These institutions have engaged in self-study, definition of institutional priorities, and effective imaging. It is more likely that particular individuals within insititutions, such as admissions officers and development officers, are slowly introducing techniques and approaches that reflect a marketing philosophy. Typically, many institutions utilize an outside consultant to aid in remedying a confined problem such as overhauling a search-piece mailing or researching reasons for declines in minority enrollments. Although many of these efforts are good and useful in themselves, and do assist institutions in remedying problems, they are stop-gap measures that are not adequate substitutes for the development of a strategic marketing plan. To develop a comprehensive marketing plan, an institution must have a committed leadership group that understands the importance of a marketing plan; cooperation and support from all segments of the campus community; and a commitment of resources in terms of monetary support.

Henry King Stanford, then President of the University of Miami, once said, "The ultimate determinant of our fate will be society's decision as to whether the services we are rendering are worth the costs our continued existence entails." It seems foolhardy for educators not to adapt information and tools the marketing perspective can provide as they attempt to influence society's decision. It is important to note that institutions of higher education are continually involving themselves in marketing. The question is not whether to do it, but how to do it effectively (Kotler & Fox, 1985).

As pressures regarding enrollment mount, either in terms of overall numbers or in terms of specific types of students such as the talented or minorities, institutions will face difficult questions regarding institutional marketing that have significant financial implications. Institutions that can compete successfully in this arena will need to employ or to hire on a consulting basis academic planners, researchers, and communication experts.

Recruiting New Kinds of Students—Financial Boom or Burden?

In a 1975 report, the Carnegie Foundation for the Advancement of Teaching identified six types of students to which institutions might turn to realize growth in enrollment. These include: part-time students, non-degree students, older students (beyond the traditional 18–22 years), graduate and first-degree professional students, women students, and minority students. As institutions strive to meet enrollment goals, they may choose to redefine programs and services to better meet the needs of one or more of these potential growth markets.

Examples abound of successful programs that have reached the populations identified above. The University of Southern California works closely with school administrators in California who want to earn a doctorate while they maintain full-time employment. The University of Maryland—College Park offers interactive videotransmitted engineering courses to employees of IBM, AT&T, and several Maryland-based engineering corporations. Goucher College promotes a program specifically geared to assist women with baccalaureate degrees to equip themselves with the science preparation they need to compete for admission to medical schools. Chatham College in Pennsylvania offers support services and conveniently scheduled classes that enable older women to earn a baccalaureate degree part-time. In examining the success of these programs, it is obvious that programs geared to these populations must be different from traditional programs in such areas as scheduling, service, or the mode of transmission.

Mayhew (1979) offered institutions some guiding principles before they embark on efforts to attract these particular new students. These principles relate to the recognition that such programs should result in individuals' improving their credentials. They should be within the spectrum of programs that afford individuals access to state and federal financial aid assistance. Programs must be conveniently scheduled, considering both time and place, and be able to be taught by a number of qualified teachers. He also offered cautions that institutional character can be affected, both positively and negatively, by the addition of new populations.

Developing specialized programs for these special populations takes time and resources, and a willingness to change or adapt curricular offerings and services. Too often institutions identify a market segment, such as returning women, and attempt to promote their enrollment without having sufficient services or relevant and conveniently timed program offerings. When institutions make such mistakes there is a cost to the institution in terms of staff and operating resources and in terms of public relations, as well as in opportunities to institute efforts in the future. Institutions that are targeting new and radically different market segments must be aware that such ventures are long-term efforts that require advance planning and a high degree of institutional support.

Internal Reallocation of Time and Resources—How Do We Invest When Demand Outstrips the Dollars Available?

Over the past decade, the scope and responsibilities of most admissions offices have dramatically changed. In addition to selecting and "processing" applicants, many admissions offices are engaging in extensive high school visitation efforts, meeting increasing demands for participation in college night programs, executing on-campus programs to generate applications as well as to influence admitted students to enroll, and coordinating large-scale direct mail campaigns. In addition, many admissions offices are involved in cultivating alumni involvement in admissions efforts, are organizing faculty and student phone-a-thons to prospective students, and are getting involved in commercial ventures such as video networks and guidebooks in order to reach students. As the scope and nature of admissions offices change, staff in this area are trying to be more accurate in assessing the effectiveness of recruitment methods. They are trying to determine whether the expenditure of funds in a particular area results in a prospective student that could not have been reached through other means, and ultimately in an enrolled student who can be successful and satisfied at a particular institution.

In one comprehensive survey, it was ascertained that on the average, admissions office budgets were allocated as follows: 54% for high school visits, 20% for direct mail efforts, 10% for on-campus programs, and 16% for print and electronic advertising (Murphy & McGarrity, 1978). It is obvious that at the time of this study, for the majority of institutions, the high school visit programs were deemed a priority. Many schools arrive at conclusions about priorities by tradition rather than through considered judgments. Over the last decade, some admissions offices have become more sophisticated in developing information systems that can identify points of contact that lead to the generation of applications and the enrollment of students. These tracking systems, together with expanded research evaluation efforts, have led some admissions offices to realign staff time and resources, and consequently, budget allocations. For example, such assessments have induced Northwestern University to reduce high school visits and place more effort on closely targeted direct mail campaigns. In another example, the University of Pittsburgh has recently refocused its recruitment dollars from the generation of additional applications to the enrollment of specifically targeted sub-populations of its admitted pool.

In the foreseeable future, the role of admissions offices will continue to include the diverse activities previously outlined. There will be increased emphasis on the evaluation of efforts, and the realignment of time and resources to optimize the use of recruitment dollars.

CONCLUSION

Institutions must be aware of the two-fold dimension of financial issues related to admissions services—the impact of enrollment on institutional revenues, and the management of office operational expenses. Whatever the reporting relationship of admissions offices, it is obvious that their functioning, their funding, and their success affect all facets of colleges and universities.

REFERENCES

Carnegie Council on Policy Studies in Higher Education. (1980). *Three thousand futures: The next twenty years for higher education.* San Francisco: Jossey-Bass.

Carnegie Foundation for the Advancement of Teaching. (1975). *More than survival: Prospects for higher education in a period of uncertainty.* San Francisco: Jossey-Bass.

Hossler, D. (1984). *Enrollment management, an integral approach.* New York: College Entrance Examination Board.

Ihlanfeldt, W. (1980). *Achieving optimal enrollments and tuition revenues.* San Francisco: Jossey-Bass.

Jenny, H.H., & Wynn, G.R. (1972). *The turning point.* Wooster, Ohio: College of Wooster Press.

Keller, M.J., & McKeowan, M.P. (1984). *Factors contributing to the postsecondary enrollment decisions of Maryland national merit and national achievement semifinalists.* ASHE Annual Meeting Paper, Maryland State Board for Higher Education.

Kotler, P. (1986). *Applying marketing theory to college admissions; A role for marketing in college admissions.* New York: College Entrance Examination Board.

Kotler, P., & Fox, K. (1985). *Strategic marketing for educational institutions*. Englewood Cliffs, NJ: Prentice-Hall.

Ludwig, M., & Stockton, K. (1987). *When projections miss their mark*. Washington, DC: American Association of State Colleges and Universities.

Mayhew, L. (1979). *Surviving the eighties*. San Francisco: Jossey-Bass.

Murphy, P.E., & McGarrity, B.A. (1978). Marketing universities: A survey of student recruitment activities. *College and University, 53*(3), 241–261.

Smith, V.C., & Hunt, S. (1986). *A new guide to student recruitment marketing*. Washington, DC: Council for the Advancement and Support of Education.

Topor, R. (1983). Marketing higher education, A practical guide. Washington, DC: Council for the Advancement and Support of Education.

CHAPTER 5

Can You Get There From Here? Assessing the Direction of Student Financial Aid Administration From a Student Affairs Perspective

Susan L. Pugh

"Cheshire Puss," she began, rather timidly, as she did not at all know whether it would like the name; however, it only grinned a little wider. "Come, it's pleased so far," thought Alice, and she went on, "Would you tell me, please, which way I ought to walk from here?"

"That depends a good deal on where you want to get to," said the Cat.

"I don't much care where—" said Alice.

"Then it doesn't matter which way you walk," said the Cat.

"—so long as I get somewhere," Alice added as an explanation.

"Oh, you're sure to do that," said the Cat, "if you only walk long enough."

—Lewis Carroll

The management of financial aid varies widely, with the basic administrative rules frequently being outlined by governmental agencies operating within a political milieu and the administrative direction being set in response to the goals of a particular institution. Although the administrative hierarchy may not dictate that the office of financial aid report to the student affairs area, the effects of financial aid systems, processes, policies, and services are felt by the majority of students in college. It is critical that the student affairs officer have a positive relationship with the office of financial aid and feel qualified to offer constructive observations related to the operation of the office and to the awarding policies of the institution. This chapter will address several issues related to the management of financial aid, including unique issues in aid management, selected contemporary issues, management tools, and evaluation techniques. It is designed to familiarize the nonfinancial aid administrator with some of the current concerns of financial aid management.

According to Lange (1983), the establishment of a financial aid office is a relatively new phenomenon. "Prior to 1958 very few separate offices of financial aid existed at postsecondary institutions" (Ryan, 1983, p. 194). Historically, aid was administered through the admissions office, but the advent of the National Direct Student Loan program in 1958 stimulated the growth of student aid. Most commonly, financial aid is located in student affairs, but it can also be housed in business or academic affairs (Coomes, 1988, p. 171).

UNIQUE ISSUES IN FINANCIAL AID MANAGEMENT

Liability

"Student Affairs administrators with responsibilities involving student financial aid must heed a wide range of federal accounting, auditing and administrative requirements" (Janes, 1988, p. 136). Unlike the case in some other areas within student affairs, the director of financial aid (and the dean) can go to jail as a result of poor administration. The technical requirements for proper management of financial aid are frequently a matter of federal or state law. The liability for poor administration by the institution can be the repayment of federal or state aid allocated to the institution and already disbursed to the students. If fraud or deliberate lack of compliance is found, the institution can be suspended from participation in the financial aid program and administrators can be prosecuted.

Fiscal Responsibility

Fiscal allocations to the various financial aid programs are frequently determined by the institution's previous record of expenditures. If monies were allotted and unspent, it is possible that future allocations will decrease. If loans are made and not collected, the institution's participation in the loan program may be suspended (Wilson, 1989). If allocations are overspent and the monies disbursed to students, the institution will be required to cover the overdraft. If students receive official award notifications that are retracted due to overcommitment, awards will require revision; funds will need to be transferred among various accounts, or awards may be reduced, possibly resulting in a reduction of student enrollments.

SELECTED CONTEMPORARY FINANCIAL AID ISSUES

Rising Costs

In an analysis of trends in financial aid, the College Entrance Examination Board (CEEB) (1985) found that the costs of all types of higher education had risen faster than other costs in the economy. With the exception of costs incurred for attendance at public 2-year colleges, the price of higher education between 1980 and 1984 escalated by a greater amount than for the 17-year period between 1963 to 1980. Since the mid-1970s, the configuration of financial aid packages has shifted in the direction of self-help, with grant aid declining from 80% to 47% of all aid, and loans expanding from 17% to 51% of all aid processed (CEEB).

Special Services

The changing demographics in many states indicate that there will be increasing numbers of minority students wishing to enroll in some type of postsecondary education (Hodgkinson, 1985). In fact, federal special services programs, such as Upward Bound, are encouraging college attendance by minority students who are as young as ninth graders. Frequently, these students are from the lower socioeconomic levels who will require significant sums of financial aid in order to attend college. Sometimes, they are the children of a "new" middle class who have had very little time to contemplate financial planning for college or even to consider postsecondary education as a post-high school alternative for their offspring.

The composition of the staff in the financial aid office should reflect the diversity of the student population it serves. Office staff should design special counseling programs in response to the needs of students requiring personal attention. Some of the groups that should be represented include high-need, first-generation minority students, adult learners returning to college, part-time students who have families to nurture and support, and students with disabilities. Students, particularly those in these groups, should be able to avail themselves of appeal procedures that allow consideration of their individual situations. The financial aid regulations provide for "mitigating circumstances," where documented, and permit the special treatment of individuals within existing guidelines dictated by the Congressional methodology, standard budget routines, and defined student eligibility criteria. Counselors should be aware of the academic support services available for these students, so that the counselors are not caught by the federal requirements related to the monitoring of satisfactory academic progress as a condition for continued receipt of financial aid.

Federal and State Student Aid Sources

Many institutions have relied on federal and state financial aid to meet the costs of needy students, and have concentrated institutional aid on filling the need "gap" or on serving "no need" students, with goals ranging from enhancing the academic profiles of the student population in attendance to successfully competing with their sister schools for academically talented students (Zelenak & Cockriel, 1986).

Financial aid dollars have increased by 23% since the Middle Income Assistance Act of 1980. However, when the rate of inflation is considered, the increase actually becomes a decline in constant dollars of 3% (Menges, McGill, & Schaeffer, 1986). With federal aid to students further declining as a result of the Reauthorization of the Higher Education Act passed in October, 1986, institutions are faced with raising scholarship and grant funds through capital campaigns and with evaluating the effectiveness of their already-existing financial aid programs.

Federal Income Tax Laws

The basic premise of student financial aid receipt is that the parents bear the primary responsibility for financing their children's college costs to the extent that they are able. Furthermore, it is the student's responsibility to earn money for college. With the new tax laws governing the reporting of some types of financial aid as income, and eliminating some of the income protection options that upper-middle income parents have used to finance their children's costs, the advisory role of the financial aid officer has expanded, and the information required to provide financial advice to nonfinancial aid recipients has been further complicated.

Legal Requirements

The administration of financial aid also includes legal interpretations with regard to the existence of a contract between the financial aid recipient and the institution, the requirements related to publishing consumer information, the collection of debts owed the institution, the verification of financial data that might have been fraudulently submitted as a part of the application for financial aid, and the appropriate release of student information to various parties. "The federal government imposes many requirements on the way institutions manage and spend funds under federal programs" (Kaplin, 1985, p. 275). Some regulations apply to all aid programs, whereas others apply to specific programs.

Student Employees

Because institutional funds for the administration of financial aid are limited, many financial aid offices rely on student workers for routine processing tasks and for peer counseling programs. The training of students to perform as paraprofessionals, and frequently as professional counselors, requires that the financial aid office maintain adequate documentation related to policies and procedures as well as possess a system for continually evaluating the effectiveness of this special type of staff person. If the college offers a graduate program related to student personnel administration, the financial aid office generally participates in the teaching mission of the school by providing a program for interns and practicum students as well.

FINANCIAL AID MANAGEMENT TOOLS

Documentation and Training

The federal and state governments provide student consumer information, legislative updates, operating manuals, technical compendia, training workshops, and staff available to answer questions by telephone.

The National Association of Student Financial Aid Administrators (NASFAA), as well as its companion regional and state associations, offers services related to legislative advocacy and staff training, information dissemination (frequently earlier than the "official" state or federal release of new regulations), and a forum for professional development and communication.

Professional Consultants

There are organizations, approved by the federal and state agencies, that (1) compute financial need and issue financial profiles on student filers, (2) sell computer-assisted counseling and financial aid packaging routines, (3) process loans for students unable to use conventional lending sources, (4) provide scholarship search services, (5) offer financial planning advice, and (6) provide college payment services expanding beyond the timeframe of an academic year. Consultants are available who possess expertise in space and fiscal management, in techniques for enhancing the office environment, or in specific areas related to the administration of the financial aid programs themselves.

Institutional Staff

The best tools to assist the student affairs officer, however, should exist right in the office of student financial aid at the institution. The performance of the staff should reflect an appropriate blend of technical expertise to implement regulations and manage complex systems, complemented by counseling skills to transform regulations into understandable and efficient delivery systems.

Systems

It is important to remember that tools should perform at the behest of the person. Mistakes cannot be blamed on the computer, nor can the limitations of certain computer programs be allowed to dictate institutional policies. Conversion to new computer systems or the replacement of outmoded telephone systems every few years should be a part of standard operating procedures rather than the result of abrupt change, which causes staff to scramble to meet predetermined deadlines in an undetermined environment.

FINANCIAL AID RELATED TO STUDENT AFFAIRS FUNCTIONS

Packaging

The basic function of the financial aid office is to deliver awards to eligible (needy and non-needy) students, using already-existing financial aid programs. This is accomplished through "packaging" various types of financial aid into one total for an individual student. Typically, any eligibility for state and federal gift aid (i.e., state scholarships and grants, Pell Grants) is first anticipated into the total, followed by outside grant (generally private) sources of anticipated eligibility. Third, academic performance or other entitlement to non needed-based aid is analyzed and translated into a dollar figure through awarding scholarship aid or various types of fee remissions. The fourth step varies, depending on institutional funding limitations and philosophy. If funds are very limited, outside sources of aid are again calculated. For example, some schools might require the pursuit of a Guaranteed Student Loan or part-time employment for a certain amount of money. Finally, campus-based federal aid (College Work-Study, Carl Perkins National Direct Student Loans, Supplemental Educational Opportunity Grant) is awarded, sometimes in combination with grant assistance funded through the college. The value of work should not be underestimated. "Part-time on-campus employment is an effective tool for enhancing student involvement" (Astin, 1985, p. 166). Amounts of aid in the various categories can differ, based on the student's eligibility for certain funds or the institution's plan to "target" monies to certain groups of students.

Research and Evaluation

It is imperative that the effectiveness of the institution's packaging philosophy and procedures undergo continuous scrutiny, in order to ensure that the institution's goals are fulfilled. Research regarding the effects of packaging should be conducted on a regular basis, as should the evaluation of services provided by the financial aid office to parents, students, faculty and staff, and donors and lenders. Unfortunately, research and evaluation are important management components that are frequently absent in the administration of financial aid. Billions of dollars on the national level have been awarded in the various federal loan and work programs, with very little research regarding the effects of self-help on student performance or of loan aggregates on students leaving college (Van Dusen, 1979). Institutions awarding scholarships have neither implemented plans to assess their impact nor completed research to ensure that the scholarship monies are being appropriately targeted (Sidar & Potter, 1978).

Counseling

Counseling services to provide information for family financial planning, and to enhance awareness of financial aid possibilities for all students, should be offered by the financial aid office. The financial aid counselor should understand the Congressional methodology for determining financial need as well as the impact of the tax laws on various types of income deferral plans and on gift aid programs. In addition to discussing possible types of financial aid available through the office, the financial aid counselor should be able to advise parents and students with regard to borrowing alternatives, the implications of borrowing, job search strategies, budgeting techniques, and investment alternatives that will yield income to pay anticipated college costs. The financial aid office should interpret its service mission broadly in order to include the counseling of students and families who may not receive financial aid from the office at all. Tierney (cited by Graff, 1986) suggested that the office of financial aid serve as a clearinghouse for student financial planning. An economist commenting on the role of the financial aid office in a college environment offered a suggestion to change the name to "The Office of Family Finance and Planning," because higher education is probably the *only* industry in the United States that sells a big-ticket item without offering across-the-board assistance with financing (Case, 1986).

Innovation

The financial aid office should be innovative in meeting the needs of students. Fund-raising responsibilities may be shared with the development office, and financial aid administrators might find it beneficial to educate other campus constituencies on issues related to financial aid (Tierney, cited by Graff, 1986). The financial aid administrator should become familiar with the technicalities of tax-free bonds to private investors as a potential source for student loans; with tuition plans for employees of corporations; with moral obligation scholarship programs, income contingent loans, and nonexpendable trust funds to cities; and with the establishment of scholarship endowments. The institution may investigate incentives related to parents' prepaying all or part of their children's costs in order to avoid inflationary increases; this would also allow the institution to invest additional capital.

The financial aid office should explore the use of new media techniques, including the development or purchase of videotaped presentations to use with students and parents and to use for staff training and development. Technical innovations should be researched, such as optical scanning devices for the entry of various financial aid data elements, new telephone systems that can be designed to transmit and accept student information related to financial aid, or personal computers for remote entry of application data or for individually directed counseling programs.

Positive Orientation

The course of financial aid management should be deliberate and refined, rather than crisis-oriented in response to abrupt changes in financial aid eligibility criteria or funding alternatives. It should be creative and innovative, rather than comfortable with the status quo. It should be service oriented from a broad perspective of serving all constituencies, rather than limiting services to eligibility interpretations and disbursal of funds. The managers should possess current research reports that demonstrate the effectiveness of the office personnel and show evidence of their innovative stewardship with the funds at their disposal.

The office should function in a generally supportive environment that should result in positive attitudes of students, faculty, and other constituencies toward the office. The communication between the financial aid office and the administrative hierarchy at the institution should be mutually satisfactory. In a survey conducted by the National Association of Student Financial Aid Administrators (NASFAA) in 1983, it was found that although 90% of the financial aid directors perceived that they had sufficient authority to function effectively, almost 25% of them were not sure how their superiors perceived their performance.

EVALUATION TECHNIQUES

Sometimes the financial aid office exists in an administrative world filled with all of the contradictions and confusions of Lewis Carroll's Wonderland. It may also seem that the domain of financial aid management particularly lends itself to multiple interpretations, so that any direction may seem to be adequate if followed long enough. Martin (1983) discussed a variety of approaches to evaluating financial aid programs.

It is important that the direction not only be defined but also be apparent to the constituencies that the financial aid office serves. If the student affairs officer has questions about the general direction or the appropriateness of the direction of the financial aid office, there are some observations that can be made independently.

1. *Proper Administration of Funds*—Audits of the federal programs must be conducted every 2 years and the results kept on file at the institution. If the institution is a member of NASFAA, a recently completed NASFAA Self-Evaluation Guide should also be on file.

2. *Appropriate Level of Professionalism*—NASFAA, as well as the regional financial aid professions, publish codes of ethics that state the general principles under which the financial aid office should operate.
3. *Available Research*—Statistical reports related to maintenance of effort, as well as various federal and state fiscal year-end reports and fund requests, should be on file at the institution.
4. *Efficiency of Delivery*—The awarding cycle of financial aid, from notification of students to disbursal of awards, should be similar to the enrollment cycle of the institution and should be planned in cooperation with the admissions office.

The best approach, however, is probably the well-known "Management By Walking Around (MBWA)" technique (Peters & Austin, 1985). Visit the financial aid office. "The most important issue in determining how an institution's financial aid office should be organized is how the aid program supports the institutional mission" (Lange, 1983, p. 235).

1. *Does the office seem to be quiet?* Then it is probably efficient and the students are happy, or there would be long lines of people waiting at the front desk and all of the staff would look harried. Of course, the students may feel so alienated that they just don't visit, and the staff so discouraged that they just don't talk.
2. *Does the office seem to be neat, with all staff either working on a task or talking with a client?* It is probably efficient and adequately staffed. Of course, staff could be sitting on all kinds of financial aid that has never been awarded and only those few lucky souls with scholarships could be visiting. Refer to the secondary documentation, such as federal audit reports and college fiscal reports.
3. *Do the application materials and information brochures make sense?* Are they complete and logical, so that students and parents can understand the services provided and financial aid available? Is there adequate information available for the faculty, academic advisors, and other student personnel professionals who work with students on campus? Is financial aid appropriately tied to recruiting? Does it reinforce the academic mission of the institution?
4. *Do you feel comfortable when you visit the office?* Do you know the professional staff members and feel that they are committed to helping students and their parents? Are the staff interested in your opinion, willing to answer your questions, able to provide the information you need? Do the students you see, in your own professional environment, seem to feel comfortable with the financial aid office and do they feel financially well-grounded at

the institution? What do students and their parents say about the quality of service?

If the observations are predominantly positive, then the financial aid office is proceeding in the right direction toward the future, and has gone "the distance" in serving the constituencies it was designed to assist.

SUMMARY

Getting there from here is never easy in the world of financial aid. There are too many intervening variables to make the trip an easy one. Strong attention to careful management and student needs, however, will make the journey much smoother for all those involved.

REFERENCES

Astin, A.W. (1985). *Achieving educational excellence*. San Francisco: Jossey-Bass.

Carroll, L. (1963). *Alice's adventures in wonderland*. New York: Macmillan.

Case, K.E. (1986). The office of family finance and planning (Formerly the financial aid office). American Association for Higher Education *Bulletin, 39*(5), 8–11.

College Entrance Examination Board. (1985). *Trends in student aid: 1980–1984*. Washington, DC: Washington Office of the College Board.

Coomes, M.D. (1988). Student financial aid. In A.L. Rentz & G.L. Saddlemire (Eds.), *Student affairs functions in higher education* (pp. 155–184). Springfield, IL: Thomas.

Graff, A.S. (1986). Organizing resources that can be effective. In D. Hossler (Ed.), *Managing college enrollments* (pp. 89–101). New Directions for Higher Education No. 53. San Francisco: Jossey-Bass.

Hodgkinson, H.L. (1985). *All one system*. Washington, DC: Institute for Educational Leadership.

Janes, S.S. (1988). Administrative practice: A day-to-day guide to legal requirements. In M.J. Barr (Ed.), *Student services and the law* (pp. 129–151). San Francisco: Jossey-Bass.

Kaplin, W.A. (1985). *The law and higher education*. San Francisco: Jossey-Bass.

Lange, M.C. (1983). Factors in organizing an effective student aid office. In R.H. Fenske & R.P. Huff (Eds.), *Handbook of financial aid* (pp. 221–236). San Francisco: Jossey-Bass.

Martin, A.D., Jr. (1983). Evaluating and improving administration of aid programs. In R.H. Fenske & R.P. Huff (Eds.), *Handbook of financial aid* (pp. 258–280). San Francisco: Jossey-Bass.

Menges, R.J., McGill, L.T., & Schaeffer, J.M. (1986). Innovations & options: How colleges cope with reductions in federal aid for students. American Association for Higher Education *Bulletin, 39*(5), 3–7.

National Association of Student Financial Aid Administrators. (1983). *A profession in transition: Characteristics and attitudes of the financial aid administrator*. Washington, DC: Author.

Peters, T., & Austin, N. (1985). *A passion for excellence: The leadership difference*. New York: Random House.

Ryan, D.R. (1983). Staffing the aid office and improving professional expertise. In R.H. Fenske & R.P. Huff (Eds.), *Handbook of financial aid* (pp. 194–220). San Francisco: Jossey-Bass.

Sidar, A.G., Jr., & Potter, D.A. (1978). *No need/merit awards: A survey of their use at four-year public and private colleges and universities.* New York: College Entrance Examination Board.

Van Dusen, W. (1979). The coming crisis in student aid: Report of the 1978 Aspen Institute Conference on Student Aid Policy. *The Journal of Student Financial Aid, 9*(1), 3–19.

Wilson, R. (1989, June 14). College and trade school officials raise questions about U.S. plan to reduce loan-default rates. *The Chronicle of Higher Education*, pp. A–18, A22–A28.

Zelenak, B., & Cockriel, I.W. (1986). Who benefits from no-need scholarships? *The Journal of Student Financial Aid, 16*(1), 20–25.

CHAPTER 6

Funding and Financial Management of Counseling Centers

Donald W. Nance

This chapter is organized around three major objectives. The first is to provide a context for understanding the financial workings of counseling centers by identifying several dimensions and distinctions important to their functioning. The second objective is to identify and discuss issues currently affecting counseling centers and to illustrate the response to these issues. The third objective is to identify the variety of funding sources for counseling centers. Each category of funding is identified and illustrated with examples. The potential issues and strategies associated with each type are discussed. Institutions specifically mentioned by name tend to be universities. No implication is intended that the issues faced or the creative funding options developed are not applicable or in use at counseling centers throughout the whole range of higher educational institutions.

The writing style is intentionally more conversational than rigorously academic. In a few cases, references are cited. However, much of what is going on in counseling centers, particularly with respect to funding, has never been formally published (Heppner & Neal, 1983). Much of the information comes from my 25 years of involvement with counseling centers, professional meetings, and networking with other directors of counseling. My understanding of funding has developed in the process of exploring funding options for the counseling center at Wichita State University, where funds are drawn from all the major categories to be discussed in this chapter. I hope the ideas presented here will stimulate thought, discussion, and creative actions on this essential topic—money.

FUNCTIONS OF COUNSELING CENTERS

If all counseling centers were surveyed in their range of functioning, funding levels and sources *would* be apparent. To provide a context for understanding the financial patterns and issues counseling centers face, it is necessary to briefly describe some of the commonalities and differences in what counseling centers do and don't do. The literature on the roles and functions of counseling centers has been well reviewed by Heppner and Neal (1983). Historically counseling centers have operated in four major areas:

1. Academic and educational counseling;
2. Career or vocational counseling;
3. Personal/social adjustment counseling; and
4. Testing.

Certain of these functions may be the shared or exclusive responsibility of another unit or department on campus. Academic and educational counseling may be done by an academic advising unit or be performed in academic departments. Career and vocational counseling may be shared with the placement center, or the placement function may be a part of counseling. Personal adjustment counseling or psychotherapy also may be offered by the mental health staff in the student health center. Testing activity may be centralized or distributed around campus. With such a range and mix of these four functions, counseling centers operate very differently depending on the degree of responsibility for each area, assigned priorities, and the degree of overlap with other units.

An additional distinction among services is important in understanding counseling center functioning. This distinction is between services offered for normal or developmental problems versus remedial or reconstructive services. Sharpening study skills and testing a student's interests to assist in selecting a major or dealing with initial adjustments to college life are responses to normal developmental problems that can be anticipated. Programs can assist students, frequently in group formats, to deal with developmental issues. On the other hand, reading at a second-grade level, severe test anxiety, changing majors for the fortieth rather than fourth time, or coping with physical or sexual abuse requires more remedial (and often more resource-consuming) services. Most student affairs professionals agree on the necessity of programs and services to meet normal developmental needs. Less agreement exists about the type and extent of remedial services to be offered (Gelso, Birk, Utz, &

Silver, 1977). One type or model of a counseling center views significant remedial services as beyond the scope of its mission and purpose. Such a center will refer to other resources or defer, that is, not get involved.

The testing function, often a part of counseling centers, is rooted in the academic training of many counseling center staff. The counseling and guidance movement led in the development of ability, interest, and personality tests as aids to the counseling process. Because counseling often used tests, the link was maintained. Today, the testing function frequently includes the administration of various national examination programs. Services not directly related to counseling, such as scoring classroom exams and operating sophisticated laser scanners, may grow out of the testing function and be included in the responsibilities of some counseling centers.

ISSUES AND RESPONSES

Given a range of responsibilities among counseling centers, are there issues common to counseling centers? If so, are there trends in how those issues are being addressed? As is the case with many questions, the answer is both yes and no. Counseling is affected by all the trends of financial accountability identified in this book, but the degree and direction of the impact of an issue vary, as do the responses to an issue. What are some of these issues and responses?

Several issues of counseling centers are common to other student affairs units. First, issues of efficiency, effectiveness, and accountability affect counseling centers (McKinley, 1980). One-to-one counseling is a relatively expensive way of providing service. Yet, individual counseling is the method in which most counseling center professionals have been trained and one they may prefer. Tension may exist between a remedial, relationship-oriented, individual approach to counseling or therapy and a more developmental, educational, group approach. The days of a counseling center staff successfully adopting a posture of "Leave us alone to do individual psychotherapy with students without having to worry about money" are over, as well they should be (Foreman, 1977).

A second issue is the merger and reorganization of activities involving counseling centers. The press for mergers comes from the desire to eliminate duplication of services by organizational consolidation. The responses to this press have varied. Counseling centers have been merged into student health centers, and vice versa, so that all mental health services are consoldiated. Counseling centers have been reorganized into units with a clear developmental, educational focus, with the mental health and remedial services being clearly assigned elsewhere (Nejedlo, Wood, Drake, & Weissberg, 1977). A few centers have been dismantled altogether as a result of severe budget reductions or failure to demonstrate effective, efficient results within the institution.

In many counseling centers, more students request services than can be served. Even with increasingly efficient methods of delivering services such as groups, videotapes, courses, and computers, the demand for services often exceeds capacity. How does a center respond fairly and effectively in the face of demand exceeding supply? One response has been to limit the amount of services a student can receive. Many centers have time limits on counseling. Mechanisms for exceeding the limits are usually based on an assessment of a client's exceptional needs. If user fees, discussed later in the chapter, are involved, more services can be provided using the fees generated. In this case service may be restricted by considerations other than money, such as limited office space.

Waiting lists are another response to excess demand. At one time, waiting list procedures were similar to those of restaurants. The student's name goes on a list, perhaps with a category of problem designation (academic, career, personal), much like restaurants put customers on a smoking, nonsmoking, or first-available waiting list. This procedure has been modified in many centers in response to another current issue— legal liability. If a person were to announce that starvation was imminent, should the restaurant still demand wating in turn? An intake procedure frequently is used in conjunction with waiting lists, so that the nature and severity of the problem can be assessed and options explored.

A trend toward clients seeking services for more severe problems has been noted in the annual data bank survey of counseling center directors. The increasing range of students in college, the availability of paid-for or low-cost quality services, and the social acceptance of mental health services may all contribute to this trend. Currently, campuses must respond to problems of eating disorders, suicide attempts, and abuse of drugs, including alcohol. Responses to these issues illustrate the need for cooperation in education, prevention, identification, and treatment of problems. Residential life, counseling, student health, and student activities all may be involved in different aspects of a coordinated response to these problems.

The multiple tasks performed in counseling centers and some of the issues currently affecting centers provide a context in which to consider the various ways counseling centers are currently funded. New combinations for funding may emerge when considering the categories of funding.

CATEGORIES OF FUNDING

Category I—Regular Institutional Allocations

The dominant source of funding for counseling centers, as for many units in student affairs, is allocated resources that flow through the institutional budgeting system. The specific features, methods, and procedures will vary among the budgeting methods discussed in previous chapters. Whatever the particular method, the counseling center is treated as a unit or department within a division or college, much the same as the English department or the office of the registrar. The budget is developed based on an identified, incremental percentage allocated to each unit within the institution. "Figure your current budget plus 5% and allocate that amount among salary raises and operating expenses" is the form of instruction given for budget preparation. Budget reductions or cuts are called for in much the same manner.

The financial management tasks for functioning within such a process are, at one level, very straightforward. The axiom is "Monitor expenditures and don't go over your budget." A corollary axiom in many institutional systems is "Be sure to spend all your budget." In many budgeting systems, funds cannot be retained or carried over from one fiscal year to another. Thus, no incentive exists for ending the year with unspent money. Staying within or under budget may be seen, in some systems, as careful stewardship; in others, it is an indication that the current budget is either adequate or too generous. Good financial management actually may involve overspending the budget so as to reinforce the perception of continuing need and to use effectively any money left from other units.

Familiarity with the particular budget capacities is critical to successful financial management of this type of funding. Which categories of the budget can be combined? Which transferred? What are the major categories of funds? Examples of major categories are:

1. **Salaries:** with subcategories of professional staff, office staff, and student assistants;
2. **Operating Expenses:** with line items such as telephone, office supplies, and duplicating; and
3. **Capital Equipment** for items such as computer equipment and office furniture.

Forming a positive, cooperative working relationship with the budget office on campus can greatly increase a counseling center administrator's efficiency and fiscal effectiveness. A cooperative working relationship can also reduce frustration and circumvent roadblocks. Asking questions like "How can [*your goal*] be accomplished?" and "What happens if [*possible action*] can yield critical information on the inner workings of the budgeting and accounting processes?" (Note that the form of the above questions asks for information and cooperation rather than rulings and restrictions.)

Category II—Program Improvement/Additional Allocation Funds

In an institutional budgeting process, these funds are not distributed routinely to all departments. Distribution is based on identified institutional needs and priorities. Typically, justifications must accompany the requests, and competition is keen at both divisional and institutional levels. Counseling centers often have difficulty competing for these funds. In most organizations the support areas follow the direct production areas in the priorities for receiving additional resources. In higher education, credit hours are a major measure of production and the major source of income. Thus, academic colleges and departments are the "production units" and frequently have priority in this type of funding.

How well the case is made linking increases in funds for counseling with the institution's academic mission and priorities correlates highly with successful competition for these funds. Connecting requests for additional funds to the priorities of the student affairs division and the institution is a key financial management strategy. For example, recruitment and retention of students may be a priority for College A with its declining enrollments, but is likely to be a much lower priority for College B, an enrollment-capped institution with four applicants for every opening. A request for an additional counselor justified on the basis of retaining students whose personal problems would otherwise interfere with their ability to continue in school corresponds to institutional priorities for College A but not for College B.

Requests for additional funds also can be strengthened by tying the request for additional support to criteria or standards external to the institution. Institutional comparisons for staffing and funding levels are useful. How are counseling centers at comparable institutions staffed and funded? Clearly the basis of comparison must be meaningful and creditable. How the counseling center at Ohio State University is funded may not carry much weight in justifying the need for another position at Norfolk State College in Nebraska. The external standards of accrediting agencies are another source of comparison or justification. The

International Association of Counseling Services is one such organization for counseling centers. How much weight such standards hold will vary with the importance placed on the standard by each institution's administrative chain of command. Certainly nothing exists comparable to the National Collegiate Athletic Association with its power to impose sanctions, or the National Council for Accreditation for Teacher Education (NCATE).

If internal priorities or external standards are insufficient sources of support, it may be necessary to identify what needs and presses are being externally imposed on the institution. Requests are tailored to meet those needs. For example, a 1989 mandate from the federal government for a "drug free workplace" requires institutional support in order to offer programs to meet this federal priority. A counseling center request for a drug and alcohol counselor to work in education, prevention, and treatment is congruent with the new need to comply with this federal mandate.

Category III—Academic and Training Funds

The funds in this category are budgeted principally for the staff to perform services other than direct counseling activities. Two examples are teaching courses that produce credit hours and supervising the counseling activities of trainees. Practicum students and interns provide counseling services to students in order to satisfy course, degree, and experience requirements.

Credit courses taught by counseling center staff most often have a significant personal development component in addition to the course's curriculum content. Academic courses can be a very cost-effective method of responding to many of the normal developmental needs of students. Topics of human sexuality, career decision making, assertiveness training, counseling skills, study skills, the freshman experience, and reading improvement are all illustrative of the kinds of courses counseling centers may staff. The counseling center at the University of California-Irvine exemplifies this pattern of activity and funding.

Credit hours generate revenue for the institution. The link between this revenue and counseling center funding may be quite direct. Institutional funding formulas developed for academic departments may be applied to the courses taught by counseling center staff. The direct application of a formula would make such funds essentially the same as funds in Category I. Because student affairs divisions and counseling centers are not academic departments, the funding for teaching activities of counseling centers may be determined by a more negotiated, less formula-based agreement. An academic affairs administrator, student affairs administrator, and director of counseling might agree on a method for providing additional money to the counseling center, enabling the center to provide staff for course instruction. The agreement might be: "Academic affairs will provide funds for two counseling positions. In exchange, each of four counselors will cover two section of Human Sexuality 101." Agreements of this type are more similar to Category II funds, or the internal contract discussed under Category IV of this chapter.

Training is the second type of activity tied to academic funding. Graduate students gain supervised experience by providing counseling services to clients of the counseling center. The professional staff of the counseling center assume the role of supervisors, often with a concurrent reduction in direct client contact. The degree of training involvement for any given center varies from none, to supervising an occasional practicum student, to a center in which almost all direct counseling services are performed by counselors-in-training.

A training-oriented center has several attractive features. Certainly, the availability of free or low-cost labor is appealing. As budgets have tightened in the 1980s, the number of counseling centers seeking approval from the American Psychological Association (APA) for their internship programs has virtually doubled in number, while the number of applications for internships is shrinking. The cost-effectiveness of interns has been analyzed and formulas proposed for determining the cost of supervision, training experiences, and units of service (Schauble, Murphy, Cover-Paterson, & Archer, 1989). The multiplier effect is a second potential advantage. Professional staff members provide one hour of supervision for a trainee who has seen 6 to 10 clients, thus multiplying the number of clients served for the hour of professional staff time. Involvement in training may also stimulate staff to stay professionally current, provide campus linkages to academic departments, and offer clients a motivated, supervised, albeit relatively unexperienced, counselor. In addition to inexperience, other disadvantages include: issues of matching the severity and type of client problem to the experience level of the counselor, maintaining the continuity and quality of programs despite a built-in turnover of counselors, and managing the conflicts between training and service needs.

Counseling centers at institutions with graduate programs in human service fields such as psychology, counselor education, and social work, may serve as training sites; counseling centers at the University of Missouri-Columbia and the University of Notre Dame are examples. If such counseling centers do not serve as training sites, a training site is likely to contend with one or more training clinics on campus; such is the case at Ball State University and Kansas University. Counseling centers at institutions with less graduate training emphasis will range widely in the level and type of training involvement. Institutions with no graduate training may be limited in the role training can play in providing counseling services.

Category IV—Grants and Contracts

Money for grants and contracts is considered soft rather than hard money. Historically hard money refers to the first two categories of funding discussed in this chapter. Hard money is firm, stable, ongoing, and dependable. Soft money is time-limited and therefore less dependable. In times of enrollment instabilities, state fiscal crises, and shifting legislative priorities, the relative firmness of the funds may be less distinct.

The process of requesting and receiving additional program improvement funds has many elements in common with developing grant proposals and negotiating contracts. The granting or contracting organization has needs, priorities, and funds. The task is to demonstrate how your organization can meet the identified needs and requirements and thereby be deserving of the funds. In the case of Category II, program improvement funds, the grantor is the central administration of the institution and the grant may be permanent. There are essential similarities in developing budget justifications and in submitting grant proposals. Just as the budgeting and controllers office are important resources for Category I & II funds, the office responsible for grants and contracts within the institution needs to be your ally in working to secure external funding.

External grants and contracts take many forms. Counseling center staffs have skills, interests, and resources that can be matched to the needs and priorities of grantors and contractors. Assisting local corporations through a program for recently relocated spouses (Preissler, 1989), or providing services to disadvantaged persons enrolled in federal programs (Cohen & Nance, 1982), can build bridges into the community, provide opportunities for staff, and provide income to the counseling center. An example more national in scope is the contract many centers had for providing testing and career planning services to veterans under contract with the Veterans Administration (VA). The VA needed assistance in counseling veterans leaving the armed services, and counseling centers had the skills and resources to help meet the need. Because college education frequently was a part of the veteran's career plans, an indirect recruitment function also resulted from the contract.

Counseling centers with a testing function often contract with the various testing services, such as Educational Testing Service (ETS), The American College Testing Program (ACT), and the College Level Examination Program (CLEP). The tenor of the times brings with it an emphasis on documentation, suggesting an increasing use of standardized testing programs for selection and certification. Groups as diverse as the Professional Golfers Association (PGA), state licensing boards, and corporations require testing. Such groups contract with counseling centers for these services. Because much of the testing for such groups is conducted on Saturdays, counseling centers have frequently been able to use the programs as a way for interested staff to earn additional income and have not included this money in the budgeting process.

Contracts also can be internal, that is, within the institution. Internal contracts can be negotiated when counseling center staff perform in areas beyond the usual scope of the counseling center. Suppose that an academic department needs course coverage and approaches the counseling center for staff to teach. Assuming such teaching is beyond the usual scope of counseling services, that additional duty could be (1) declined, (2) performed gratis—no funds allocated or transferred, (3) performed as an overload with the staff member receiving the additional compensation, or (4) negotiated as an internal contract. Essentially, the contract has counseling staff assigned to teach as a part of their center duties, and the academic department agrees to transfer money to the budget of the counseling center.

On some campuses, the relationship between the residence life unit on campus and the counseling center includes an internal contract for services. The residence halls may want and need counseling center staff dedicated to working in staff training, consultation, and outreach in residence halls. The counseling center cannot provide sufficient staffing from Category I funds. An agreement to build counseling funds into the residence life budget can meet the needs of both residence life and the counseling center.

Category V—Fees

Fees come in a variety of forms and exist for any of a number of reasons. Some fees are mandatory—everyone in the group is assessed—whereas others are user fees paid by anyone using a particular service. The distinction is similar to the distinction between roads constructed and maintained from general revenues and toll roads, where the fee is collected from those who use that particular road. Mandatory student fees exist at nearly every college and university. Such fees may be assessed for general or specified use. A user fee usually is designated for a specific purpose, such as freshman orientation. A request-based budgeting process usually exists to allocate general student fees. A mandatory fee may be dedicated to the counseling center. At Colorado State, for example, all funding comes from student fees. No Category I or II money is involved. A mandatory student fee provides most of the budget. User fees are assessed for ongoing individual therapy. The user fee for therapy generates revenue but also serves to limit services and to encourage utilization of more efficient services.

User fees for service open the possibility of receiving funds for service from a third party insurer. If the clinical services provided, such as group or individual therapy, are covered by health insurance, procedures can be established for billing insurance companies directly. A multitude of issues accompany entrance into the world of health care insurance. Issues of record keeping, confidentiality, the qualifications of the service provider, and necessary diagnostic labeling are all inhibitors to recovering insurable charges. Exploring how procedures are set up at local community mental health centers, student health services, and medical schools can provide insight into relevant state statutes and customary fees. Counseling centers at the University of Cincinnati and Wichita State University both have been engaged in collecting insurance payments for several years. Discussions with counseling center directors indicate an increase in centers considering user fee options.

The University of Texas, among others, has adopted another response to the insurance issue-referral. Students in need of psychotherapeutic services beyond the scope or limits of the counseling center may be referred to private and public resources in the community. Health insurance, including the student health policy, then can be used by the student to help defray the costs of treatment.

Several issues arise in fee-base funding and deserve special mention. Obviously student fees may raise the overall cost of education to students. When do fees become burdensome? In the University of North Carolina system, fees have more than doubled in the last 10 years (113%), while tuition has risen at a much slower rate (41%) (Fees outpacing tuition, 1989). A second issue relates to which services should be included and paid for via tuition or legislative appropriations and which activities go beyond those the institution is obliged to provide and should be funded by fees or not supported at all. Other relevant considerations such as competition with the commercial business sector are covered in chapter 8.

Category IV and V funding carries the risk of reducing the likelihood of additional regular funds. Responses may be, "If you need more computers, more staff, or additional programs, raise more money from your other sources" (Category II) or, "Because you are doing so well with alternative funding you don't need this money, so it will be reallocated to the more needy" (Category I). If funding from Categories I & II is currently marginal and prospects for significant improvement are dim, then little is really at risk when alternative funds are pursued. An agreement for "benign neglect" may be useful. Something like, "The counseling center understands that additional funding is unlikely. We will actively pursue alternative sources of funding. If we are successful, don't cut our regular funds. In that way, the center, the institution, and the students can benefit from our extra efforts."

SUMMARY QUESTIONS

When considering how a counseling center is currently funded and operated and what options are viable for the future, several questions can be helpful in guiding those considerations.

1. COUNSELING FUNCTIONS AND FUNDING
What is the counseling center currently doing?
- What is the mix of the four major functions?
- What priorities exist within the center?
- How effectively and efficiently are those priorities implemented?
- What is the center relationship to other units within student affairs, the institution, and the community?

How adequate is the current funding?
If funding from regular institutional sources is ample, the priority is on the effective use of those funds.

A related priority should be maintaining the visibility and institutional position to protect continued funding and serve the needs of students.

If the funding from the regular sources (Category I) is marginal to inadequate, the rest of the questions are very important.

2. INSTITUTIONAL CLIMATE
- What is the current financial situation of the institution?
- What trends are likely to affect the institution? With what effects?
- What are the institutional funding priorities? Where is the counseling center in those priorities?
- What current or emerging institutional needs could the counseling center meet in order to be a funding priority?

3. ALTERNATIVE FUNDING SOURCES
How will alternative funds affect regular funding?

- What are the skills, resources, and services the center has to offer?
- Who has needs for those services and who will pay?
- How will alternative funding affect the center's overall function and funding? (If income generated is a priority, then paying clients and services become priorities as well.)

The answers to these questions, along with the questions raised in the reading of this chapter and book, can be aids to the thoughtful approach to financial management.

REFERENCES

Cohen, P.M., & Nance, D.W. (1982). *Postsecondary student services for CETA participants.* American Council for Education Monograph. Washington, DC: American Council on Education.

Fees outpacing tuition. (1989, July 2). *Greensboro News and Record*, pp. C1–2.

Foreman, M.E. (1977). The changing scene in higher education and the identity of counseling psychology. *The Counseling Psychologist, 7*, 45–47.

Gelso, C.J., Birk, J.M., Utz, P.W., & Silver, A.E. (1977). A multigroup evaluation of the models and functions of university counseling center. *Journal of Counseling Psychology, 24*, 338–348.

Heppner, P.P., & Neal, G.W. (1983). Holding up the mirror: Research on the roles and functions of counseling centers in higher education. *The Counseling Psychologist, 11*, 81–98.

McKinley, D.L. (1980). The counseling center. In W.H. Morrill & J.C. Hurst (Eds.), *Dimensions of intervention for student development*. New York: Wiley.

Nejedlo, R.J., Wood, G.L., Drake, W.M., & Weissberg, M. (1977). A good trip: From counseling center to counseling and student development center. *Personnel and Guidance Journal, 55*, 257–259.

Preissler, S.M. (1989). A student affairs corporate partnership. *Journal of College Student Development, 30*, 279–289.

Schauble, P.G., Murphy, M.C., Cover-Paterson, C.E., & Archer, J. (1989). Cost effectiveness of internship training programs: Clinical service delivery through training. *Professional Psychology: Research and Practice, 20*, 17–22.

CHAPTER 7

Financial Management of Student Health Services

Scott T. Rickard and *Debra Benoit Sivertson*

Student health is in the midst of a revolution, according to nationally recognized experts in the profession (Califano, 1986; Fuchs, 1986). This revolution, or paradigm shift, involves the nature of funding of health care as well as who delivers the services. In this chapter we focus on issues, trends, and alternative funding approaches for student health services. The purpose is to provide information and perspective on the financial management of student health. Because student health typically reports to student affairs, the relationship between the chief student affairs officer (CSAO) and director determines how effective student health will be in meeting the needs of students and other constituents. The different roles, responsibilities, and perspectives of directors and CSAOs can result in consensus or conflict on issues of funding, staffing, or program priorities. Accordingly, we have incorporated both points of view, acknowledging that differences exist, and if both are willing to share information and establish a relationship of mutual trust, then student affairs, student health, and the university will be the beneficiaries. Our study also embraces the reality of diversity within the over 3,200 accredited institutions of higher education. Diversity characterizes the delivery and funding of health services. With this understanding in mind, we will examine various funding approaches, identify potential benefits or liabilities from various vantage points, and make explicit our preferences and identify the basis for those judgments.

IDENTIFYING THE CRITICAL QUESTIONS

Student health represents a microcosm of health-related issues in the larger society. The growing complexity of health problems confronting student affairs and student health professionals, coupled with escalating costs of providing services, places added importance on exploring financial options. The "business as usual" approach of the traditional health services will not be adequate to the task of responding to increased health care needs of students with problems such as alcohol and other drug use and misuse, HIV/AIDS and genital human papillomavirus or other sexually transmitted diseases, date rape, sexual abuse, anorexia, and bulimia. Creative funding approaches will be necessary in order to respond to these and other health concerns, such as the increasing diversity of the student population.

The unique characteristics, history, and circumstances of each institution of higher education argue against proposing a universal model for funding student health services. However, each institution, regardless of size, setting, or budget considerations, needs to address similar questions in determining its overall financial approach. The central question concerns the mission of the institution and its role within the community. If the mission involves service to the community, then health services may be designed differrently. The nature and extent of health services in the community also influence the on-campus program. What services are available in the community? How close are they to campus? How far away is emergency care? Are there HMOs, local providers, public health clinics, sliding-scale opportunities for care, or other institutions of higher education? Considering these questions helps determine the level of care that may be influenced by community resources and the convenience of these services. However, an institution in an urban setting with the availability of optional services may decide that duplication of services is best for its students.

The nature of the student body is an equally important consideration in shaping the institutional health program. The mix of residential and commuter students is one important characteristic of the student body. For example, residential students of traditional college age and those living close to campus without parents typically seek health care two or three times a semester. This contrasts with the commuter student who may not seek care at all or only once during a semester. On the other hand, the commuter student may seek more health care information, because even in large urban areas with several health care alternatives, these services are often not available, at least not at a reasonable cost.

The task for student health and student affairs administrators is to examine funding alternatives with the knowledge of community resources and the characteristics of the student body. A funding approach for student health must also consider whether students should pay a separate fee and whether the institution will contribute resources. Funding decisions for student health need to be conducted in the context of the total costs of educational programs and services. The costs of funding student health need to be an integral part of a total budget plan for all services rather than a separate, isolated item. This approach maximizes effective use of fiscal resources in support of students but also, with respect to student health, views health services as an integral component of retention. Unhealthy students cannot be truly successful students. Many students will leave the institution due to serious illnesses, not having had the benefits of prevention or early intervention. Moreover, the critically important concern with community health cannot be overlooked, as shown by the institutional costs of responding to measles epidemics on several campuses. Creative ways of funding health care should be made after a comprehensive evaluation of needs and resource options in contrast to viewing student health as a separate fiefdom unaffected by institutional forces.

Regardless of the particular configuration of programs and services, quality of care remains a guiding concern. Institutions must make the commitment to meet standards of the American College Health Association (ACHA) or ambulatory accreditation bodies (Accreditation Association for Ambulatory Health Care, 1985a). Quality of care, as defined by the ACHA (1984) standards, indicates that "services must be provided in a manner consistent with the principles of professional practice and ethical conduct, and must reflect concern for cost involved" (p. 5). However, the student as consumer may have a more limited and specific definition of quality of care. The accreditation process or consultations may assist institutions in reviewing issues concerning quality of care.

Student Health Services Audit

The CSAO and director of student health need to have a common understanding of student health. One approach is to audit programs and services jointly. The authors conducted a national study utilizing the audit checklist approach (Rickard & Sivertson, 1989). The list of 20 questions rank-ordered, from highest to lowest, the CSAOs' knowledge of student health services. For example, the two items that CSAOs had the most knowledge about were compliance with standards and the mission statement. Conversely, the least knowledge was demonstrated on commitment to do outreach and whether a needs survey had been conducted. Moreover, a national study of chief student affairs officer perceptions of student health identified health education and outreach as the two areas that needed the most improvement (Rickard, 1987). The study clearly shows the need for CSAOs to establish a systematic way of obtaining timely information and evaluation of health services programs and services. Rickard and Sivertson's 20 questions appear below.

1. *Is care provided in compliance with standards?* Has a self-study, actual accreditation visit, or consultant visit taken place to see if the health service is in compliance with ambulatory, and infirmary, if appropriate, standards for college health and other ambulatory care areas where applicable?

2. *Is there a mission statement?* Is there a written mission statement that is consistent with the institutional statement?

3. *Is there a scope-of-practice policy?* A statement that clearly defines the kind of services offered and professionals who provide those services is needed. The scope must reflect the capability, resources, and legal guidelines for professionals. The statement should be consistent in all materials, that is, catalogues, handbooks, and brochures.

4. *Is there staff development?* Staff development should include documentation of updates for current issues, have a clear policy, reflect quality assurance issues, and be funded.

5. *Does the care include health education?* Health education should be incorporated into all levels of care from patient visit, telephone contact, and actual programming.

6. *Do you know what the quantitative measures are?* Quantitative measures must include a clear definition of such areas as visits versus contacts, telephone contacts, outreach efforts, time spent in each. The ACHA has developed a microcomputer-based program that can be used by any size health service to assist in managing this information in a consistent manner for the field.

7. *Is there collaboration with the campus community?* Collaboration with the campus community includes joint programming with other institutional areas, sharing expertise and referral, representing health concerns where needed, and including the community beyond the institution for referrals for students and other agencies. Programming for and with outside community groups will depend on the institutional mission statement and resources.

8. *Is the level of care consistent?* Care should be given within an established scope of practice by competent providers in compliance with the mission statement and standards. Care should be consistent throughout student health services; that is, each provider follows similar guidelines for the history, physical evaluation, diagnosis, and education for bronchitis. Level of care can be evaluated by quality assurance standards.

9. *Are there procedures for complaints and suggestions?* Is there a systematic way to gather, document, and respond to complaints and procedures? Does the chief student health officer know if there are any trends? Are concerns addressed about quality assurance when appropriate?

10. *Have there been evaluations of services?* Is there a consistent evaluation of health services, for example, by a questionnaire to users and nonusers, with follow-up of issues raised?
11. *Are resources based on needs?* Has there been a needs evaluation taking into account student body resident versus commuter, community resources, kinds of students, financial resources, and priorities attached, or are services offered in response to an individual's priorities?
12. *Are there mechanisms for student/consumer involvement?* Is there an active student health advisory committee, peer educators, or student government association liaison, and are their suggestions taken seriously and are they supported by student health services staff?
13. *Is there collaboration with the external community?* Are there either informal or formal liaisons with community agencies such as the Heart Association, Lung Association, and other groups?
14. *Do resources complement community resources?* Are the health services programs coordinated with those of the community, or do they overlap or replicate them? Have conscious decisions been made to coordinate services?
15. *Is there evaluation of the efficiency and effectiveness of staff patterns and type of staff?* Have the job descriptions, level of skill, type of education, and scope of practice been evaluated to identify the best staffing pattern for cost effectiveness, efficiency, and care?
16. *Are resources based on the mission statement?* Can student health services fulfill the mission statement effectively and well with the resources allocated?
17. *Are quantitative measures clearly defined?* All institutions are number-driven—GPA, SAT, student-faculty ratios and the like. How are statistics reported in student health? Beyond knowing what the data measures are, they must be defined and used consistently; for example, a visit—a one-to-one encounter with a provider with documentation in a medical record; contact—a member of a presentation to a group of students on community health issues, for example.
18. *Is outreach part of the mission statement?* Does the mission statement include outreach to campus or outside community?
19. *Is there a commitment to do outreach?* Are the staff willing to do outreach and do they have the skills, including interpersonal, organizational, and educational skills, to do so?
20. *Has there been a needs survey?* Has an acutal survey of the needs of the campus population been completed for services including health education? Is care provided in compliance with standards?

In summary, the audit checklist provides a means for periodic review of student health services prior to allocation of funds. It provides the CSAO and director with "a joint tool for evaluating and renewing relationships, assessing knowledge of student health, and evaluating the existence and vitality of programs" (Rickard & Sivertson, 1989, p. 211).

Funding Approaches

The funding of health services in higher education is as varied as the institutions they represent. Seven different approaches, based on the funding source, have been identified as follows: 100% allocated funds, 100% student fee, combination of allocated funds and student fee, student fee plus health maintenance organization (HMO) subscribers, mandatory health insurance, fee for service, and contract for service. In addition, self-help is one additional cost-effective approach that has been used in providing health services. For example, self-help units have been established for colds or minor cuts.

A brief description and discussions of the pros and cons of the various approaches follow. Pros and cons depend on the perspective of the observer, whether director, CSAO, chief business officer, chief academic officer, chief executive officer, or student. Each approach has potential strengths and weaknesses. Moreover, whether a particular funding approach is viewed favorably or unfavorably depends on individual views on the nature of institutional commitment, accountability, control, flexibility, and cost-effectiveness, to name a few of the more important dimensions.

1. 100% allocated funds. Funded from the general budget, this approach provides a strong institutional commitment to student health, typically covers overhead costs, and provides a relatively stable source of funding (except in times of budget reductions). Cost-effectiveness and establishing priorities for services are also features of this funding approach. Depending on the perspective, this funding source requires student health to compete with academic and other student services for a "piece of the budget pie." It has greater budget scrutiny than most other approaches, has less flexibility, and makes student health programs vulnerable to budget reallocation. For example, long-term health education programs are vulnerable to budget reductions in order to maintain clinical services. Also, inflation adjustments typically don't match increased medical costs, but consumers continue to expect the same level of service. Health services at William Jewell College, the University of Richmond, and Central Missouri State University have utilized this approach.

2. 100% student fee. Health services funded entirely from student fees and consumer charges typically operate as auxiliary services. Some auxiliaries pay all expenses, others pay only rent, and some do not pay for facilities or any other hidden costs including benefits. The auxiliary service feature increases flexibility, as with the use of reserve funds. From the director's perspective, budget control and flexibility are advantages. From the CSAO's perspective, a health fee also increases flexibility of funding for other nonfee-supported services. A student fee provides accountability to the consumer, requires better marketing and closer ties with student advisory groups, and affords a more direct relationship between costs and services. Potential liabilities include: all indirect costs must be paid, such as electrical, heating, billing, and other administrative costs; increased costs for salaries and inflation are covered from the fee, which erodes the base annually; increased fees to meet needs obtained by generating support are vulnerable to budget reductions if enrollment declines. Health services can be held hostage to the need to minimize the total cost of education for students. An example is the increased use of comprehensive fees to fund several student services versus increasing tuition. Because there are never enough funds to cover the needs of all student services, the temptation to raise the fee beyond the need and divert funds for other services raises the specter of ethics in budgeting. If this approach is taken, students should be informed that fees earmarked for student health are being used to support other services. Health services at the University of Virginia, Old Dominion University, the University of Florida, and Wesleyan University have used the 100% student fee budget approach.

3. Combination of allocated funds and student fees. This approach to health services funding includes both allocated funds and student fees. Fee support ranges from 10% to 90%. The advantages of this combined funding approach include a balance of commitment from the institution and students. Using two funding sources increases budget flexibility, reduces susceptibility to the vagaries of enrollment-driven budgets, and tends to minimize budget fluctuations. One potential problem of this approach occurs in tight or declining budget cycles. Fees may be increased to redirect other funds—a zero-sum game from the perspective of student health. When fees are increased but not services, the student perception is, "We're paying more and receiving less." This funding approach requires greater student involvement, which can be a benefit. Health services at Brown University, the University of Maryland-Baltimore County, and the University of California at Berkeley have used this approach.

4. The health maintenance organization (HMO). Health services operating as an HMO also may have funding from several sources, but the key difference is the level and type of subscriber. Community members of all ages are included as subscribers, which provides a larger budget base and range of services. Funding includes premiums paid from third-party coverage. The advantages of this approach include: broad range of services for students; broader funding base; community involvement; and significant accountability. Potential problems with HMOs are: higher up-front costs and less priority of service for students; students can end up bearing the cost for a population with more illness, for example, the elderly; reduced flexibility and less control because of outside involvements; and being subscriber-driven. Health services at Harvard, Yale, and the University of Massachusetts-Amherst have utilized this approach.

5. Health insurance. These operations have mandatory health insurance programs and rely on these policies to pay for services generated in the community as well as on-campus. Advantages of the health insurance approach include: flexibility; creative funding; fewer or no charges once in the system; coverage for referrals of students off-campus resulting in better management of staff time. Potential disadvantages are: accountability may be more external; students pay up front regardless of need or use of health services; and it may be more costly for students. Also, the underwriter, or insurance company, may "drive" the health program by virtue of what it will pay for rather than the needs of students. Illness prevention programs can be at risk.

Policy options vary depending on the nature of the coverage. Three such options are primary coverage, coordinated coverage, and excess coverage. Under the primary coverage approach, the insurance benefit may pay for the first dollar of coverage and for all costs within the limits of the benefit structure. The second type of reimbursement strategy can be called "co-insurance" or coordinated insurance. In this scheme, benefits of more than one policy are coordinated according to terms specified in each policy. A student with college-provided insurance and other insurance would receive benefits based on a coordinated structure of reimbursement. In the excess coverage approach, the policy makes a payment only after all other applicable insurance resources are exhausted. It also pays "first-dollar" in circumstances where no other insurance exists.

Student health insurance can participate in the review and planning for insurance options from the role of buyer and broker or vender. In the buyer/broker role, health services designs an insurance benefit package to provide insurance protection for students who will be acquiring health services and incurring reimbursable costs entirely outside the structure of direct care provided at the college health center. From this perspective, institutions that require and also provide insurance operate as buyers and brokers of insurance on behalf of students. Institutions use the collective buying power of a group of beneficiaries to acquire insurance protection for that group at reduced costs.

In the second role, health services acts as a vendor of benefits with reimbursable costs. The insurance benefits acquired for students may also reimburse the health service when services include a benefit that has a charge and is also reimbursable under the insurance plan (Burns, 1985).

6. Fee for service. Under this approach, health services relies primarily on payments for each service. Some services may be coordinated with health insurance plans so that students can utilize the policy. Otherwise, students are billed or must pay when they are seen. From the director's perspective, this approach provides maximum control, much like running a private office. It also has minimal cost to the institution. Possible disadvantages include: may undercut the spirit of college health, particularly health education and student development; very little institutional commitment or involvement; lack of flexibility; lack of funds for health education and outreach; limited accountability; and the student carrying the full burden of costs. Also, if the staff are not seeing patients, they are not generating revenue. The University of Louisville has operated under this approach.

7. Contract for services. Some universities have contracted out partial or total health care services for students to outside agencies such as HMOs. Service arrangements vary and can include services both on and off campus. The potential advantages of this approach are: less cost to the institution; basic health care needs are met; and less responsibility by the institution. This approach has several possible disadvantages: may undercut the spirit of college health, particularly health education and student development; lack of control and accountability (a contract with an outside agency limits control over quality of care, the values and interpersonal skills of providers, and knowledge of developmental issues of college age groups); lack of institutional commitment; less emphasis on health education and outreach; lack of student input in services; lack of involvement of health care staff with institution; lack of knowledge about what's happening with student health issues; and issues of student development not being addressed. The University of San Francisco and Bard College have operated under this approach.

In summary, the preferred funding approach for a particular institution depends on the mission, objectives, philosophy, values, and funding options available. From the perspective of the CSAO or health services director, issues of control, flexibility, and accountability need special attention in weighing the alternatives. Assuming the availability of several options, a combined approach provides the most stability.

Regardless of the approach, health service directors need sufficient budget flexibility, such as through a revolving fund, for response in the case of health emergencies.

FUNDING LEVELS

What are the funding levels of student health services for various kinds of institutions and funding approaches? The American College Health Association's Network guide provides one data source for answering such questions. Table 1 summarizes the range and median costs per subscriber for 200 institutions in the ACHA 1986–87 report. The table uses the 1987 Carnegie classification system. For all institutions, the median costs per subscriber were $56. Median costs were greatest in Research I and Research II institutions at $100 and $94 respectively. Doctoral I and Doctoral II institutions also were above the median cost, as were LA I colleges. All other categories were below the median. The large range of costs within each institutional category, with the exception of 2-year schools, suggests that a number of variables influence the level of costs for any one institution.

Table 2 shows the median costs of three of the most prevalent funding approaches from the 1986–87 ACHA Network guide. All but four of the 186 student health services were funded by one of the three approaches—100% allocated, 100% student fees, or a combination of the two. All three had a wide range of costs per subscriber. The 100%

TABLE 1
Student Health Services Subscriber Costs by Carnegie Classification

Carnegie Classification	Number of Institutions	Cost per Subscriber	
		Range	Median
		(in dollars)	
RES I	33	24–433	100
RES II	17	18–257	94
DOC I	15	8–217	81
DOC II	18	20–481	58
COMP I	71	3–127	31
COMP II	12	9–147	38
LA I	26	17–324	76
LA II	8	5–119	53
TOTAL	200	3–481	56

RES = Research; DOC = Doctoral degree-granting; COMP = Comprehensive; LA = Liberal arts.

TABLE 2
Student Health Services Subscriber Costs by Funding Approach

Funding	Number of Institutions	Cost per Subscriber	
		Range	Median
		(in dollars)	
100% allocated funds	72	3–481	33
100% student fees	71	6–341	68
Combination	39	16–353	63
Total	182		

allocated funds approach was approximately half as costly per subscriber as the other two models.

TRENDS

Although student health services are as variable as their host institutions, there are clearly identifiable trends that can affect the financial planning and management of programs and services. The trends include the following:

1. *Institutions continue to close infirmaries and redirect space and funds to health education and other programs.* Institutions have discovered the increasing cost and liability of infirmaries and the decreasing availability of nurses. This has raised questions regarding funding for infirmaries. The increased interest of health services personnel in student development and educated consumers has caused funds to be redirected toward educational activities. More proactive procedures and tools to assist students in cooperation with other campus areas and community have developed, for example, a holding bed in an area emergency room, or a single room in housing if a student has the chicken pox and cannot go home.

2. *Students are increasingly being referred to community facilities for after-hour care and admission.* More and more health services are arranging after-hour care with community services. On-call phone triage systems by health center personnel—registered nurses, nurse practitioners, physician assistants, and physicians—have proven to be successful staffing arrangements.

3. *Insurance issues have become more complex for the providers of health care, affecting the funding of college health.* Health insurance has changed greatly. More institutions have indicated interest in mandatory insurance. Policies are now being developed to complement health services

care based on student needs versus what companies decide to provide. Health service directors need to be more involved in the process of developing bid specifications and selecting the policy. Too often the process is controlled solely by the business office, with little or no involvement of student affairs and student health services. Moreover, CSAOs need to be familiar with the recently developed ACHA standards for insurance (American College Health Association, 1988).

Some states have deleted health professionals' malpractice coverage for public institutions, which increases the cost to the employee or health service. Providing malpractice coverage is an important benefit in an increasingly competitive marketplace and should be considered in the funding of benefit packages.

4. *Because of the increased complexity of student health service operations and budgeting, directors are becoming increasingly involved in management activities.* Directors at institutions of all sizes are finding themselves more involved in administration, policy setting, and evaluation. Adequate training and time are necessary. Job descriptions should reflect these changes, and personnel with these qualifications as well as staff development training monies must be identified.

5. *Advertisements for director positions are more generic and less focused on the MD model.* Directors are assuming more managerial duties and are increasingly being advertised generically. Such individuals as nurses, nurse practitioners, physicians, MBAs or MPHs, and holders of other master's degrees may fit the qualifications. Searches have been more skill-driven than degree-driven.

6. *The use of nonphysician providers is becoming more commonplace. Nurse practitioners have proven to be cost-effective and provide quality care.* Nonphysician providers such as nurse practitioners, physicians' assistants, and other nurses and health educators are being used to provide the staff mix to meet the scope of practice and educational needs.

7. *The nursing shortage has seriously affected college health.* The nursing shortage is well documented in an ACHA study (1989b). The report indicates that the nursing field has been characterized by rapid turnover, recruitment problems, and a decline in the quality of applicants. One suggestion mentioned in the study is that student health hire more nurse practitioners with an increased emphasis on health education. Salary, benefits, creative advertising, and other recruitment methods have become major issues and require CSAOs' knowledge of market values and trends.

8. *Health education, once considered a luxury, has become an essential component and a key focus of student health services.* Health education is the essence of college health. HIV/AIDS, HPV, other STDs, anorexia, bu-

limia, high cholesterol, stress, and other health concerns have made prevention the key. Colleges who have relied on providers in the community to take care of students' sore throats, injuries, or other medical care have quickly realized what's missing—health education. Education is, after all, the purpose of higher education institutions. The "fix and send them out" attitude can no longer be accepted.

9. *There is an increased emphasis on wellness and empowering students as knowledgeable consumers.* Providing the student consumer with knowledge and skills to enhance the quality of life, and consumer knowledge of rights and responsibilities, has become a guiding philosophy of health care and a central philosophy of health services. With such issues as HIV/AIDS, HPV, high cholesterol, and abuse of alcohol or other drugs has come the realization that students must be taught the skills to make decisions for risk reduction. The developmental issues of experimenting with sexuality and learning responsibility and autonomy carry higher risks today. Health education programs must provide methods to help students develop skills (i.e., self-esteem building, assertiveness, problem solving/decision making, stress reduction, and negotiation) and teach ways of assessing these personal skills. Health center peer programs and other health education efforts need to use these components to assist students in successfully reducing their risks for disease and therefore increasing the long-term quality of life. Education regarding the health care system, when to seek care, how to evaluate insurance programs, and how to provide self-care should also be included in educational programs for students.

10. *Issues such as HIV, AIDS, alcohol and other drug abuse, HPV, and anorexia and bulimia also have increased the need for staff development.* These issues require increased knowledge in order to recognize and evaluate these problems and to provide services or referral for affected individuals. Financial support and time must be provided so that staff can effectively meet these challenges. In addition, encouraging the director and the staff, particularly in small health services, to join ACHA individually as well as institutionally is an excellent way to enhance current information about college health.

11. *CSAOs, increasingly concerned about the costs of health services, need to explore a variety of funding and staffing options.* CSAOs looking to contract out health services and do away with health services on an "all or none basis" first need to clarify priorities and services. For example, on some campuses, CSAOs and student health services directors must jointly reexamine programs and services in relation to limited resources and consider redefining the scope of practice. These joint decisions may necessitate making choices between two desirable options or focusing priorities on

particular groups. For example, should the scope of practice be narrowed to use more specialists in community health, or should limited resources be directed to an in-house gynecologist consultant?

12. *The "standards movement" influences the delivery of student health services as well as other areas of student services.* Although college student health did not participate in the development of the Council for the Advancement of Standards (CAS) standards for student services/development programs, CAS endorsed the standards of the American College Health Association, currently under revision. CSAOs should utilize standards to help ensure quality of care and make health services more accountable. Consequently, CSAOs need familiarity with ambulatory standards (Accreditation Association for Ambulatory Health Care, 1985a) in order to work closely with directors in reviewing programs and services.

13. *Increasingly, issues of diversity affect financing of student health.* These include health concerns of international students, date rape, HIV/AIDS, homosexuality and homophobia, and stress related to race and gender. With respect to international students, a joint report of ACHA and the National Association for Foreign Student Affairs (1989c), *Optimizing Health Care for Foreign Students in the United States and American Students Abroad,* provides a highly useful reference for reviewing the health needs of international students.

14. *Computers are used increasingly in management of college health programs and services.* Computers have helped health administrators manage data and be more cost-effective. For example, mandatory immunization policies need a computer data system to help ensure compliance. The ACHA has provided updated guidelines for immunization policies and procedures (ACHA, 1989a). Financial resources are needed to provide the technology and training so that health professionals can monitor health care more effectively and efficiently.

In summary, these trends illustrate the increasing complexity and importance of student health services. They also have obvious implications for the funding of services and programs.

REFERENCES

Accreditation Association for Ambulatory Health Care. (1985a). *Accreditation handbook for ambulatory health care* (1985–86 ed.). Skokie, IL: Author.

American College Health Association (ACHA). (1984). *Recommended standards and practices for a college health program* (4th ed.). Rockville, MD: Author.

American College Health Association (ACHA). (1988a). *Standards on student health insurance.* Rockville, MD: Author.

American College Health Association (ACHA). (1988b). *Update: Immunization.* Rockville, MD: Author.

American College Health Association (ACHA). (1989a). *Nursing personnel survey: The effect of the nursing shortage on college health.* Rockville, MD: Author.

American College Health Association (ACHA). (1989b). *Optimizing health care for foreign students in the United States and American students abroad.* Rockville, MD: Author.

Burns, W.D. (1985, June 1). *Restating the case for mandatory student health insurance.* American College Health Association annual meeting, Washington, DC.

Califano, J.A. (1986). *America's health care revolution: Who lives? Who dies? Who pays?* New York: Random House.

Fuchs, V.R. (1986). *The health economy.* Cambridge, MA: Harvard University Press.

Rickard, S.T. (1987). Perceptions of health services by student affairs officers: Is the partnership healthy? *Journal of American College Health, 35*(4), 153–157.

Rickard, S.T., & Sivertson, D. (1989). Auditing the wellness of student health services: Is your student health service healthy? *NASPA Journal, 26,* 207–211.

CHAPTER 8

Auxiliary Enterprises: Running a Business Within an Institution

Michael S. Noetzel and *James A. Hyatt*

Colleges and universities today have become innovative and adept at offering services to both students and the campus community that at one time were offered only by private sector businesses. "Doing it themselves" has helped many institutions dramatically cut costs and provide services tailored to meet the specific needs of their campus.

Sound financial management of the auxiliary areas of colleges and universities is essential to the fiscal health of the institution. Because auxiliary enterprises provide services, either directly or indirectly, to all segments of the campus community including students and alumni, faculty and staff, and in many cases, residents of the local area, exposure to and involvement with these services is unmatched by other campus operations. This responsibility, however, entails difficult issues for campus administrators involved with managing and setting policy for auxiliary enterprises. This chapter discusses some of the key current and future issues of auxiliary operations and offers ways to manage campus auxiliaries within this environment effectively.

AUXILIARIES AS PART OF THE CAMPUS COMMUNITY

As is true of any successful partnership, a clear understanding by both parties of their respective responsibilities is essential. For example, auxiliary operations have a right to expect quality support services, such as plant operation and maintenance, from the parent institution. In addition, the cost of such support services should be at a rate lower or equivalent to that of external vendors. In a similar manner, colleges have a right to expect high-quality service from their auxiliaries. In both cases, the realization of such expectations results from good communication. For example, if the services provided to auxiliaries are substandard, the director of auxiliaries should raise this concern with the campus business officer. It is then incumbent upon the business officer either to rectify the situation or to offer an alternative solution.

Colleges also have several expectations with regard to the quality of auxiliary services. The quality and level of services provided by auxiliary operations, for example, can be an effective incentive for recruiting and retaining students. Many auxiliaries have recognized this fact and have structured their services to meet student needs. Student food services, for example, are offering a variety of meal plans and, more importantly, offering students a variety of choices in food, from hamburgers and hot dogs to deli sandwiches. In addition, college stores, through effective merchandising, have become a "one-step" shopping alternative by offering everything from textbooks to microcomputers. A listing of potential auxiliary services is included in the appendix (Barnett, 1987).

TRENDS IN INSTITUTIONAL MANAGEMENT OF AUXILIARIES

In most organizations, among the principal management activities are *planning, budgeting, control,* and *evaluation* (Koontz, O'Donnell, & Weihrich, 1984). In order to carry out these activities effectively, cooperation among all elements of the university community is essential. "Planning and budgeting are intricately interwoven and have closely related, mutually supporting roles" (Coleman, 1986, p. 58).

In planning and budgeting, accurate estimates of revenues and expenditures are essential. If actual expenditures are greater than projections, a significant reallocation of existing resources may be necessitated. Also, if expenditures are not monitored carefully, an institution could experience a deficit at the end of the year. In this regard, an ongoing system of budgetary controls is essential if managers are to react promptly to budget variances instead of waiting until the last minute to take corrective action. Finally, a comprehensive evaluation of institutional and auxiliary operations at the end of the fiscal year helps identify problem areas or areas of opportunity. Such information facilitates corrective action and improves the accuracy of future plans and budgets.

With escalating tuition and fees and increased competition for students, colleges and universities need to be more sensitive to the needs of students. Managers of auxiliary services, for example, have a responsibility to solicit input from students or other clients on the efficiency and effectiveness of the services provided. Administrators need to share this feedback with other campus departments and ensure that the central administration is aware of areas where services should be modified or expanded.

Recent budget reductions have also altered the student's role in the auxiliary service area. For example, services that previously had been supported or subsidized by institutional general funds, such as day-care programs or health services, are now dependent on student fee revenue. Please note chapter 7 on health services for a more complete discussion of this issue. As the burden for support has shifted more to the student, students are expecting more of a say in how these programs should be run and the range and quality of the services provided. For example, at Indiana University, all room and board fees must be approved by the Halls of Residence Committee, which includes a substantial number of students. The Memorial Union Board Administrative Advisory Committee at the University of California, Davis, reviews bid proposals on food service, and advises the chancellor on activity rate structure and budgetary priorities. Five undergraduates serve on the committee. Campus administrators should work with students in order to make them better informed and more responsible decision makers.

Importance of Modern Management Techniques

Campus administrators responsible for auxiliary services have access to an increasing array of management techniques. Four of the most widely used management techniques are: (1) cost accounting; (2) planning—both strategic and long-range; (3) alternative budget strategies; and (4) cost center and responsibility center management.

1. *Cost accounting.* In order to be successful, an enterprise must not only maximize revenue generation, but also reduce or contain operating costs. Cost accounting helps managers to achieve these objectives first by identifying costs, and second, by examining the impact of alternative costing policies. For example, in the early 1980s the State University of New York at Buffalo conducted a survey of student housing costs. When institutions were asked whether their housing operations were self-supporting, the majority of respondents indicated that they were. However, when they were asked whether they covered only direct costs, such as salaries and other operating costs, or both direct and indirect costs, the majority of respondents indicated that only direct costs were covered. When indirect costs, such as administrative support (e.g., accounting, personnel, purchasing, etc.) were included, the number of self-sup-

porting housing operations dropped dramatically. It is important, therefore, that auxiliaries understand the full cost of providing services. By collecting such information, they can readily identify high-cost areas and attempt to contain or reduce costs. In addition, cost data can also be useful in establishing fees for auxiliary services.

2. *Planning.* Auxiliary services, like private businesses, can be successful only if they establish objectives and develop plans for their operations. In the last several years, colleges have used a management technique called strategic planning. Strategic planning is useful for identifying institutional objectives and for examining alternative ways of achieving them. Alternative ways of providing housing could include leasing unused space in the community such as motels or apartment buildings, or negotiating with other colleges that have excess dormitory space. In the fall of 1988, the University of Louisville, for example, leased motel space when demand for campus housing exceeded available supply.

The University of California, Davis, has embarked on an innovative land-use plan under which the university will lease 10 acres of land to private developers at a price of $1 per year for 50 years. The developer will then build housing units for use by university students. Under the plan, the ownership of the land will revert back to the university at the end of the 50-year lease (Staff, 1988).

In terms of revenue generation, strategic planning helps to identify ways of increasing sales. For example, according to the National Association of College Stores Merchandising/Operating Survey, combined sales for college stores posted an 11.2% increase in sales volume during the 1984–1985 school year. A major factor in this growth was attributable to the broadening of college store product lines.

Long-range planning also helps an organization to look beyond the scope of current operations and to establish long-term objectives. For example, a college may be concerned that auxiliary services, such as food service and housing, are underutilized in the summer months. By developing a long-range plan for addressing this problem, such as using the space for summer conferences, an institution may be able to turn a problem into an opportunity.

3. *Alternative budget techniques.* A good manager is not content with perpetuating the past but is more interested in asking "what if" questions. For example, what if the department's operating budget were increased by 10% or what if it were reduced by 5%? With the advent of microcomputers and spreadsheet software, such as Lotus 1-2-3, it is now easy to "model" different management scenarios. In addition to this technique, known as alternative level budgeting, other innovative budgeting techniques exist. Incentive budgeting, for example, allows a manager

who is able to reduce costs or increase revenue to retain a portion of these savings. The manager then can use the funds to help improve operations either by buying new equipment to improve services or by exploring alternative ways of generating additional revenues, such as adding a new line of merchandise in the bookstore. Further descriptions of alternative approaches to budgeting are discussed in chapter 1.

4. *Cost centers and responsibility centers.* In order to control costs and provide operating units with increased flexibility, a number of colleges have established cost centers or responsibility centers. Under a cost center approach, an auxiliary enterprise, such as a bookstore or a department within a bookstore, can be designated as a cost center. In this instance, all costs associated with this unit are identified and monitored. Many colleges have found that the use of cost center management has helped to contain and even reduce operating costs by identifying and addressing high-cost areas.

In a similar vein, responsibility center management goes further than cost center management by assigning responsibility to the unit manager not only for controlling costs, but also for generating revenue or providing additional services.

In deciding on what management technique to employ, it is important that the problem to be addressed be clearly identified. In this regard, communication between the business officer and director of auxiliaries and their various campus constituencies is essential.

CONTRACTING AND NEGOTIATING AGREEMENTS FOR AUXILIARY SERVICES

In order to keep costs down and service high, a number of colleges have chosen to contract for such auxiliary operations as food service and college stores. Care should be taken, however, that the service an external contractor provides is equivalent or better than that provided by in-house personnel. In this regard, it is important to use management techniques, such as cost accounting, to evaluate the current costs of auxiliary operations and compare them to the costs of contracting externally. In addition, techniques such as strategic planning can help managers determine whether they are literally "giving away the store." Frequently, a strategic plan can help turn a deficit into a profit. For example, when administrators at a small college in Pennsylvania analyzed the operation of their vending services, they found that vendor income was approximately $100,000 a year, although the college received only $14,000. When the college was unable to negotiate a more equitable arrangement with the vendor, it decided to operate its own vending services. As a result of this change, in-house vending services realized a net profit of $55,066 in its first year of operation.

Another way to reduce costs and generate extra revenue is to negotiate agreements with outside businesses who wish to operate concessions or provide customer services on campus. A number of banks, for example, are interested in placing automated teller machines on campus. Such machines provide a service to students, but they also can generate additional revenue for the banks. Negotiations with a number of banks for the right to operate automated tellers on campus, therefore, can frequently result in highly favorable arrangements for colleges. Similar approaches also can be used with other companies such as fast food operations or other merchandisers.

As is true of all agreements with external groups, contracts or agreements must be carefully scrutinized and evaluated. Assistance of legal counsel is not only helpful but advisable. In addition, sound agreements result when both the business officer and the director of auxiliary services concur on the following points: (1) that customers are adequately served; (2) that equipment and facilities are adequately maintained; and (3) that services are responsive to changing student needs.

Although the challenges for campus administrators involved with managing auxiliary enterprises are great, the need to provide quality service at a reasonable cost is essential to the fulfillment of higher education's role and mission. Sound and creative management of auxiliaries on campus, in an environment that fosters effective communication between financial officers, auxiliary administrators, and the campus community in the planning, budgeting, and evaluation process, is therefore essential if higher education is to respond adequately to the current and future challenges it faces.

MAJOR ISSUES FACING CAMPUS AUXILIARIES

Unfair Competition

Revenues from college and university auxiliary enterprises have nearly doubled since 1977, increasing to approximately $9.5 billion in 1984–1985, according to a report commissioned by the National Association of College Stores (NACS, 1986). The fact that institutions are generating income from auxiliary activities has prompted charges of unfair competition by various groups external to higher education. The Small Business Administration (SBA) has been the most vocal, and specifically has noted several areas in which it considers colleges and universities to be competitors including all phases of audiovisual activity, analytical testing, consulting, on-campus travel centers, research services, and computer services (U.S. Small Business Administration, 1984). In the view of the SBA, colleges and research organizations are some of the worst offenders because they usually pay no taxes but enjoy the benefits of reduced postal rates and exemption from federal trade laws, minimum wage rates, and other insurance requirements.

On a more local level, an educational institution in the Midwest angered community businesses when its computer services, including the sale of software and hardware at discount prices, were viewed as directly competing with local computer centers. A large public university, which harbors some 20,000 bicycles and runs a repair shop on campus, has heard loudly and clearly from the local business community that bike equipment should not be sold in the campus shop. One university was sued by local interests that charged unfair competition when the institution rented dormitory rooms at less than hotel prices to guests attending an annual state festival. "Enterprises that are reasonably related to the prime educational mission of the institution have been upheld (*Villyard et al. v. Regents of the University System of Georgia*, 1948) and do not constitute unfair competition. Additionally, if the institution has statutory authority to provide services to those not directly affiliated with it, it may do so (*University of North Carolina v. Town of Carrboro*, 1972)" (Barr, 1988, p. 253). Barr concluded that court decisions have been based on several factors, including the legal authority of the institution to engage in the enterprise, the nature of the goods and services rendered, and the rationale for the college to engage in the enterprise (p. 253). These are just a few examples of the ongoing scrutiny of college auxiliary enterprises, and any legal decisions would have national implications for colleges and universities engaged in similar practices.

Unrelated Business Income

Complicating the matter of unfair competition is the issue of unrelated business income. Whereas dealing with the competition question may be something that can be addressed on an institutional level and often left to the campus's discretion, unrelated business income has national implications. The generally accepted determinant of what constitutes unrelated business income (UBI) for colleges and universities is income that is not related to the educational mission of the institution. In the future, the Internal Revenue Service (IRS) may keep even closer tabs on unrelated business income reporting in an attempt to further clarify the definition of UBI. It is worth noting, however, that as yet no college or university has had its tax-exempt status revoked for generating unrelated business income.

The issues of unrelated business income and unfair competition have attracted the attention of many state legislatures. In North Carolina, Arizona, and Illinois, public educational institutions are not permitted, by state law, to engage in any revenue-generating activity that is not related to their educational mission. Several other states are considering similar laws. A significant result of this type of legislation is the further distinction between public and independent institutions. Only public institutions have been restricted by their state legislatures from this type of activity; independent institutions are restricted only by their own decision making as to which activities they choose to pursue.

Several colleges and universities across the country are developing policy statements on competition with private sector businesses to fit their individual campus situations. Such statements take into consideration the ethical implications of engaging in competitive activities, the impact on community relations, the financial cost and benefit, and the institutional need for various services.

The IRS definition of unrelated business income also should be carefully considered by colleges and universities in order to ensure that appropriate taxes are being paid. Institutions should recognize that no tax rate is 100%, and that even when paying taxes, additional income still should be realized. Finally, college and university administrators should review and stay current on IRS rulings and information in order to make determinations on how the IRS will treat unrelated business income in the future.

The National Association of College Stores (NACS) recommends that colleges and universities consider legal and financial restructuring by separating their research and teaching functions from revenue-producing auxiliaries to help avoid challenges from the IRS and local business, as well as increase income and improve management (NACS, 1986). Alternatives to institutionally controlled or leased management of auxiliaries include cooperatives, for-profit or nonprofit subsidiaries, or foundation approaches. According to the 1986 NACS report, over 40% of the institutions surveyed had introduced some form of financial restructuring, and some 33% had considered a change in their legal and corporate structures.

A White House Conference on Small Business also studied the issues of unfair competition. This conference passed a resolution calling for Congress and the state legislatures to consider prohibiting tax-exempt organizations from competing with private business and to review the criteria for awarding tax exemptions (Jaschik, 1986). Increasing review of the fair competition issue will undoubtedly place greater pressure on colleges and universities to justify new and existing revenue-generating auxiliary endeavors.

Liability Insurance

Another key issue facing auxiliaries is the recent national crisis in the insurance industry, which has created severe problems for many colleges and universities. All insured areas of college and university operations, including auxiliary services, are affected by the current market situation. Campuses across the country are continuing to have great difficulty obtaining basic and umbrella liability insurance, including liability insurance for directors and officers, and liquor liability coverage. If coverage is available, the cost is exorbitant, thus causing a severe drain on college resources that could be used in supporting the basic mission of higher education. Many institutions have reported that their auxiliary organizations have paid from two to three times more for insurance, and that auxiliary operations have been unsuccessful in buying excess coverage.

In response to the crisis, colleges and universities have addressed the problem in a variety of ways. Solutions have included self-insurance, group purchasing efforts, cooperatives, creation of captive insurance companies, and development of consortia arrangements. These mechanisms have proved a temporary solution for several institutions, but many colleges and universities are still "going bare"—living with normally unacceptable exclusions or paying excessive costs. Although these solutions have provided immediate relief, the problem is such that a long-term answer, national in scope, is required.

Diminished Federal Support

Many major sources of federal funding for higher education are derived through the U.S. tax code. The Tax Reform Act of 1986 "... absolutely changes the rules of the game in higher education finance" (Andersen & Meyerson, 1987, p. 2). For example, tax-exempt bond financing has played a crucial role in providing student loans and money for facilities construction on college campuses, especially to finance auxiliary facilities such as dormitories. Subsequent changes in the tax laws that restricted the overall volume of tax-exempt general obligation and revenue bonds severely limited the unrestricted availability of this financing mechanism. Clapp (1987) provided an example. "If the dormitories include a cafeteria run by a private contractor, and cafeteria revenues exceed 10% of dormitory revenues, the bonds issued to finance the dormitory are probably not eligible for tax-exempt status" (p. 34). Restrictions on institutional use of these bonds has affected the capital replacement and renewal efforts of colleges and universities. These changes, coupled with the fact that federal support for facilities construction and renewal has all but evaporated in the last 15 years, raises the question: Should income from auxiliaries be used to reduce potential losses of federal and state support?

Increased appropriations for federal and state student aid also may increase access to higher education in some states, which could place greater demand on institutional auxiliary services. For example, if enrollments at an institution increase, new students may also choose to live on-campus, which could require additional residence hall space and dining accommodations. Conversely, if enrollments decline, a reduction in auxiliary operations may result. Services ranging from campus parking to transportation operations may be affected. A great number of funding and enrollment management issues affect the policy development and planning for auxiliary services on campus.

Increasing Costs of Education

As a consequence of these political and economic issues, the philosophy of individual campuses toward auxiliaries also may enter a state of flux. Key questions as to whether the primary mission of campus auxiliary enterprises is to provide a service or generate revenue will continue to affect institutional decision making. As trustees, presidents, and chief business officers try to hold the line on tuition hikes, many campuses will have to make tough decisions on additional revenue-generating mechanisms and the innovation required to control tuition costs. Furthermore, campus auxiliaries are being recognized more and more as an important tool in recruitment and retention efforts.

When the costs of housing as well as food services rise off campus, students look for these services on campus. Recently, higher education has witnessed a significant increase in on-campus housing occupancy rates. This trend has grown nationally over the last decade. As a consequence, campuses need to adapt continually to meet the needs of an increasing on-campus population. As more students choose to live on campus, the need for cost-effective and innovative campus auxiliaries to support that operation will be greater.

Other Issues

Other serious questions facing campus auxiliary administrators, especially in large metropolitan areas, will be how best to provide high-quality and low-cost services in a high-cost market. Questions related to employee relations and labor negotiations, especially for campuses that have unionized personnel, will remain on the horizon. One major university's concept for a microcomputer-costing program for labor negotiations, which allows union and university contract proposals to be costed out at the bargaining table, provides an effective example of innovation in this area. The need for alternative solutions to the asbestos problem that would be cost-effective yet safe will plague many institutions as they plan for replacement and renewal of campus facilities. These issues, when viewed collectively, present a challenging picture for campus auxiliaries and those who manage them.

REFERENCES

Andersen, R.E., & Meyerson, J.W. (1987). Editors' notes. In R.E. Andersen & J.W. Meyerson (Eds.), *Financing higher education: Strategies after tax reform* (pp. 1–8). New Directions for Higher Education No. 58. San Francisco: Jossey-Bass.

Barnett, R.H. (1987). Auxiliary services: An emerging force on campus. *College Services Administration* (Journal of the National Association of College Auxiliary Services), *10*(3), 30–33.

Barr, M.J. (1988). Facility management. In M.J. Barr (Ed.), *Student services and the law* (pp. 245–259). San Francisco: Jossey-Bass.

Clapp, D.C. (1987). Tax reform and the bond market. In R.E. Andersen & J.W. Meyerson (Eds.), *Financing higher education: Strategies after tax reform* (pp. 33–40). New Directions for Higher Education No. 58. San Francisco: Jossey-Bass.

Coleman, J.W. (1986). Planning and resource allocation management. In H. Hoverland, P. McInturff, & C.E. Tapie Rohm, Jr., (Eds.), *Crisis management in higher education* (pp. 53–61). New Directions for Higher Education No. 55. San Francisco: Jossey-Bass.

Jaschik, S. (1986, September 3). Small business seeks laws to bar competition from tax-exempt organizations. *Chronicle of Higher Education*, p. 90.

Koontz, H., O'Donnell, C., & Weihrich, H. (1984). *Management*. New York: McGraw-Hill.

National Association of College Stores. (1986). *Corporate structural alternatives in higher education: Matching form with function*. Oberlin, OH: Author.

Staff. (1988, September). FYI: UC-Davis partnership with developer boosts housing stock without depleting capital funds. NACUBO *Business Officer*, n.p.

U.S. Small Business Administration. (1984). *Unfair competition by non-profit organizations with small business*. Washington, DC: Author.

SUGGESTED READINGS

Burch, K. (1985). *Unfair competition in the states.* Washington, DC: Business Coalition for Fair Competition.

Frances, C. (1985, March/April). Why tuition keeps going up. *AGB Reports.* Washington, DC: Association of Governing Boards.

Hyatt, J.A. (1983). *A cost accounting handbook for colleges and universities.* Washington, DC: National Association of College and University Business Officers.

Hyatt, J.A., Shulman, C.H., & Santiago, A.A. (1984). *Reallocation: Strategies for effective resource management.* Washington, DC: National Association of College and University Business Officers.

National Association of College and University Business Officers. (1982). *College & university business administration* (4th ed.). Washington, DC: Author.

Rush, S.C., & Crane, E.E. (1986). *Corporate structural alternatives in higher education: Matching form with function.* N.p.: Coopers & Lybrand (U.S.A.), and the National Association of College Stores.

APPENDIX

Potential Auxiliary Services

1. Food Service, Contracted
2. Food Service, Residence, Self-Op
3. Food Service, Cash, Self-Op
4. Cookie Stand
5. Ice Cream Shop
6. Candy Shop
7. Bakery, Retail Shop
8. Bakery, Production
9. Vending, Contracted
10. Vending, Self-Op
11. Amusement Games, Contracted
12. Amusement Games, Self-Op
13. Beer Clubs
14. Night Clubs or Bars (Full Alcohol)
15. Student Unions/Campus Centers
16. Faculty Clubs
17. Faculty Dining
18. Laundry, Contracted
19. Laundry, Self-Op
20. Laundry Machines, Coin-Op
21. Bookstores, Self-Op
22. Bookstores, Contracted
23. Newsstands
24. Press, University/College
25. Print Shops
26. Duplicating Service
27. Word Processing
28. Copy Machines, Coin-Op
29. Typing Service
30. Typewriters, Coin-Op
31. Office Machines Repair Service
32. Housing, Student
33. Housing, Faculty
34. Housing, Married Students
35. Post Office
36. Mailing Service
37. Banks
38. Check Cashing Service
39. Airports
40. Transportation, Air Service
41. Transportation, Ground Service
42. Bus Service
43. Motor Pools
44. Travel Service/Agency
45. Van Rentals
46. Parking Garages, Pay
47. Parking Lots, Pay
48. Recreation, Indoor
49. Recreation, Outdoor
50. Recreation, Camps
51. Bowling
52. Golf Courses
53. Billiards
54. Swim Center
55. Skating Rink, Ice
56. Skating Rink, Roller
57. Arenas
58. Bike Shop, Sales/Rental
59. Sporting Goods Store
60. Photo Shops
61. Gift Shops
62. Concessions, Athletic
63. Concessions, Other
64. Ski Lodge Operation
65. Telecommunications
66. Computers, Coin-Op
67. Computers in Dormitories
68. Computers, Rentals
69. Microcomputers, Food Service
70. Microcomputers, Bookstores
71. Microcomputers, Housing
72. Radio Station
73. TV Station
74. Furniture Repair Service
75. Insurance, Student
76. Central Stores
77. Day-Care Centers
78. Conferences, Summer
79. Conference Centers
80. Real Estate

From: Barnett, R.H. (1987). Auxiliary Services: An emerging force on campus. *College Services Administration* (Journal of the National Association of College Auxiliary Services), *10*(3), p. 33. Reprinted by permission.

CHAPTER 9

Evaluating Financial Management in Student Affairs

George D. Kuh and *Elizabeth M. Nuss*

In most colleges and universities, powerful academic units receive a disproportionately high share of resources (Pfeffer & Salancik, 1974). According to Harpel (1978) and Pembroke (1985), student affairs budget requests usually receive more scrutiny than those of academic units because student services historically have been justified more on idealistic and humanistic grounds than on tangible evidence of results (Scott, 1978). If it could be demonstrated, for example, that the financial support given to student affairs could be used instead to reduce the average class size from 20 to 15 students, many faculty would argue that the benefits of smaller classes would outweigh those achieved by student affairs units (Dressel, 1973). To maintain present levels of support, it may become even more important to demonstrate the effectiveness and efficiency of student services (Douglas, 1983; Hammond & Thompkins, 1986; Pembroke).

The Carnegie Council on Policy Studies in Higher Education (1980) predicted that students will be the center of campus attention during the next few years. "Never before have the needs of our institutions of higher education and the desires of student personnel professionals been more consonant" (Kauffman, 1984, p. 35). Even if such optimistic scenarios do not eventuate, monitoring and evaluating financial management will remain important to a healthy student affairs organization. How are decisions and judgments made about student affairs budget allocations? Is resource allocation always based on cost-benefit and cost-effectiveness estimates? Or are political considerations, personal influence, and exchanges of incentives equally important (Georgiou, 1973; Tonn, 1978; Wildavsky, 1974)?

In this chapter we suggest some ideas for monitoring and evaluating the effectiveness of financial management in student affairs. First, textbook financial models are described that outline how financial management should be done. We present some reasons why such models may not be appropriate for use in student affairs. An alternative framework is described, the not-for-profit (NFP) model, which provides a better fit with accountability expectations consistent with the service-oriented mission of student affairs. The chapter concludes with a checklist for monitoring and evaluating financial management in a division of student affairs.

HOW FINANCIAL MANAGEMENT IS "SUPPOSED" TO BE DONE

The importance of rigorous program review and evaluation procedures is emphasized in many financial management models such as incremental budgeting, formula budgeting, zero-based budgeting, performance budgeting, and planning, programming, and budgeting systems (PPBS) (Caruthers & Orwig, 1979). Most of these models have some elements in common. For example, the models incorporate a time perspective. Budgeting and program planning are usually prospective activities undertaken prior to a fiscal or program year. Management controls and program evaluation may occur during a particular budget cycle (formative) or after the cycle is completed (summative) (Vinter & Kish, 1984).

Traditional approaches to financial management, like orthodox theories of organizational behavioral, describe how things should work rather than how things do unfold (Kuh, 1983). For example, PPBS, zero-based budgeting, and formula budgeting models are attractive conceptually because they emphasize linear, rational thinking and action (Meisinger & Dubeck, 1984); however, for various reasons, they are rarely used as financial management controls in institutions of higher education (IHEs).

Definitions

Several concepts used throughout this chapter require definition: efficiency, effectiveness, cost-benefit, cost-effectiveness, direct costs, indirect costs, and program review and evaluation (Meisinger & Dubeck, 1984).

Efficiency is one of the two criteria (the other is effectiveness) used for judging the performance of a budget unit such as a division of student affairs or department of residence life. Indices of efficiency are usually used in a comparative rather than an absolute sense and commonly take the form of a ratio of outputs to inputs or the ratio of the work done or energy developed by a machine, engine, or process to the energy supplied to it. An organization that produces a greater amount of output, product, or profit with the least amount of input resources is considered to be the most efficent (Anthony & Young, 1984). For example, an efficient leadership development program involves large numbers of students in low-cost training experiences.

Effectiveness refers to the relationship between a unit's outputs and objectives. The greater the contribution of outputs to the accomplishment of a unit's objectives, the more effective the unit is considered to be (Anthony & Young, 1984; Meisinger & Dubeck, 1984). An alcohol education program is instituted and at the end of the year the number of alcohol-related discipline cases is reduced by 20% and residence hall vandalism has also declined. The CSAO concludes that the resources allocated to the educational program seem to be contributing to the accomplishment of the goals and that the alcohol education program is effective.

Cost-benefit analysis refers to the processes and procedures used to produce, in comparable dollar terms, justification for the uses of resources for specific activities and results (Vinter & Kish, 1984). A CSAO determines that 40% of the students using the student employment office find part-time jobs and earn three to four times more than the actual cost of operating the service. The CSAO concludes that, from cost-benefit perspectives, the service represents an appropriate investment of resources.

Cost-effectiveness originated with the U.S. Department of Defense in the 1960s (Thompson & Fortess, 1980) and refers to the process or technique for choosing among given alternative courses of action on the basis of cost and effectiveness in attaining specified objectives (King, 1975). For example, which of three approaches to learning skills improvement (individual tutoring, computer-assisted instruction, credit courses) is most effective? If a CSAO finds that the combination of credit courses and computer-assisted instruction was less expensive than individual tutoring and that participants demonstrated greater proficiency on several measures, the course/computer-assisted instruction combination would be considered cost-effective. Forbes (1974) and Peterson (1986) suggested how to compute cost-effectiveness indices.

Direct costs refer to costs or expenses that can be readily identified with a particular service or program, such as personnel costs (salaries) for instruction or printing costs for orientation program brochures (Meisinger & Dubeck, 1984).

Indirect costs, sometimes called overhead expenses, refer to costs required to provide a service or activity that is typically shared by several units, such as utilities and accounting services (Vinter & Kish, 1984). On most campuses the costs associated with providing payroll services or utilities are budgeted and paid for centrally rather than billed to individual units. These costs do not appear on the unit's budget but must be considered when determining the actual costs of providing a service or activity (Meisinger & Dubeck, 1984).

Program review and evaluation refers to the processes used to determine whether program objectives are appropriate and whether the organization is attaining these objectives in an effective manner (Anthony & Young, 1984; Conrad & Wilson, 1985). When a CSAO wants to determine to what degree the orientation program is contributing to the overall enrollment management goals of the campus (Hossler, 1984), the CSAO may conduct a review of the orientation program. The actual processes used may vary; one approach would be to invite a team of two orientation directors and an admissions director from comparable institutions to conduct a site visit to study the program and make recommendations.

Are the Formal Models Helpful?

Although formal, rational budget controls are common to almost all colleges and universities, finding examples of institutions or units where budget decisions are based on scientific or empirically derived cost-benefit indices is difficult. For many reasons, generating accurate cost-benefit indices or measures of efficiency and effectiveness is generally not cost-effective! Decisions are often based on anecdotal information, the persuasive influence of the chief student affairs officer, or the perceived political or symbolic importance of the program or service (Wildavsky, 1974).

Why is it so difficult for student affairs to develop the "hard data" thought to be necessary for budget justification? The nature of student affairs work contributes to the problem. Costs of many student services are driven by student head count, not full-time equivalent (FTE) student ratios as are many other campus budgetary allocations. For example, at most institutions, approximately three part-time students are needed to equal the same amount of tuition revenue produced by one full-time student (Frances, 1985). Typically, increased volume reduces costs (e.g., credit-hour costs for undergraduate courses with a large enrollment are lower than costs for low-enrollment graduate seminars). However, in student affairs, some costs increase even when volume increases. For example, security costs usually increase when more students live on campus because social cohesion and a sense of belongingness may erode as the sense of anonymity increases (Balderston, 1974). In addition, most student affairs units do not have sufficient technical expertise to analyze direct and indirect costs or to assess either short- or long-term contributions of student affairs programs and services to the institutional mission. The full benefits of programs may not become apparent until years after the student has graduated.

Another reason it is so difficult to obtain cost-effectiveness measures is that the requisite comparative data often require "institutional oranges" to be weighed against "institutional apples." Which units are comparable and in what ways? Is the financial aid office best compared to admissions ... or to disabled student services ... or to career services? It is possible, of course, that a chief student affairs officer who devotes the amount of time necessary to obtain cost-benefit or cost-effectiveness indices may not have time to attend to other equally important tasks such as leadership across the student affairs division and student advocacy. One or more segments of the campus community—students, faculty, alumni, or parents—will probably disagree with the results of any cost-benefit or effectiveness analysis. The potential loss of support and confidence of these groups makes efforts to produce cost-effective indices not very cost-effective!

If cost-benefit and cost-effectiveness analyses are so difficult to generate, what can a student affairs manager do to justify the student affairs division's share of fiscal resources and to remain accountable? Many of the principles associated with financial management are typically influenced by or derived from practices used in business or industry. The not-for-profit segment offers new views and models that may be useful for institutions of higher education (IHEs) in general, and student affairs units in particular.

NOT-FOR-PROFIT ORGANIZATIONS AS AN ANALOG FOR STUDENT AFFAIRS

Like IHEs, not-for-profit organizations (NFP) are dedicated to optimizing the transfer of program resources to the intended beneficiaries or clients (students, faculty, parents, etc.) (Vinter & Kish, 1984). The process of optimizing the transfer of resources implies a value orientation. It is not surprising, then, that values play an important role in budgetary and related tasks, and that the resource allocation and management process will invariably involve conflicts and dilemmas between competing "goods."

Characteristics of NFP Organizations

The "product" or goal of NFP organizations is to provide services. Other characteristics include: the absence of a profit measure; a tendency to be service-oriented; unclear technologies (Cohen & March, 1974) and constraints on goals and strategies; less dependence on clients for operating resources; self-directed, autonomous professionals as employees; governance structures different from the for-profit sector; the importance of political influence; and, finally, a tradition of inadequate management controls (Anthony & Hertlingzer, 1980, p. 31). Several of these characteristics are particularly important for IHEs. For example, Anthony & Hertlingzer emphasized that the absence of a single, satisfactory measure of performance comparable to the profit measure is the most serious management control problem. Without a profit measure, comparisons of performance between disparate units performing dissimilar functions are not possible.

Constraints on goals and strategies exacerbate the comparison problem in IHEs. It is usually easier for a corporation to decide to sell or dismantle an out-of-date division that is no longer profitable than for a college or university to eliminate an existing degree program. A CSAO might decide that the provision of free or subsidized legal services is no longer consistent with the institution's goals or mission. However, the CSAO cannot unilaterally implement the decision. Before a decision can be implemented, the consumers and other relevant constituencies—students, alumni, parents, and others—expect to be consulted.

The role of the governing board also differs from board action characteristic of a profit corporation. NFP board members are selected to represent the public interest, are not likely to be compensated for their time, and tend to have less prestige and influence than the governing boards of profit organizations. Trustees are seldom appointed by those responsible for the organization. The role of the NFP board member is challenging because her or his personal judgments must take the place of profit measures in making decisions about efficiency and effectiveness (Anthony & Hertlingzer, 1980).

Performance by NFP organizations must be measured differently than profit-oriented organizational performance because the superordinate goal is to render as much service as possible within resource constraints. In most NFP situations, the ideal is to break even. Among the difficulties that arise in attempting to measure NFP performance are multiple objectives that cannot be readily expressed in quantifiable terms. In addition, members of the management team may not agree on the relative importance of the various objectives. Most CSAOs have experienced the frustration associated with determining budget priorities for the campus or institution. At some level, everyone is committed to institutional goals—teaching, research, and service. Nonetheless, unanimity about specific budget priorities is often impossible to achieve.

Types of NFP Organizations

Anthony and Hertlingzer (1980) provided a useful framework for thinking about student affairs functions as NFP organizations. They described three NFP types: (a) the business-like organization, (b) the fixed-resource organization, and (c) the fixed-job organization.

The activities of business-like organizations are similar to those of profit-oriented businesses. A substantial portion of revenues are derived from client fees. The organization is able to determine, or at least influence, the amount of available revenue and expenses incurred. Residence halls and dining services have counterparts in the profit sector. Revenues are realized from room, board, and other user charges. The level of expenses incurred can be determined by the type and scope of services and facilities offered. The goal is to respond to client or consumer preferences and to be competitive in the market.

Business-like student affairs units, such as the bookstore, residence halls, health service, or food service, generate a considerable amount of revenue. Typically, revenue estimates are best made by accountants using recent-year revenue levels and information about trends and policy changes that might influence revenue. For example, state policy might permit NFP units, such as university bookstores, to solicit students during registration but not allow privately owned bookstores to solicit on campus. If this policy were changed to preclude campus solicitation by all bookstores, including those run by the university, a university's bookstore could realize a decrease in expected revenue.

In fixed-resource organizations, resources for a given year are predetermined or fixed by a budget allocation; fees for service and other client charges are not allowed. The fixed-resource organization cannot spend more than the amount allocated. The dean of students office, financial aid, and some career services units can be considered as fixed-resource organizations. The amount of the allocation is based both on the perceived need for, and quality of, services and the amount of resources available. For example, the relative quality and importance of services supported by United Way are considered within the context of the amount of funds raised in the previous year and available for allocation. Campus budgetary allocations to most student affairs units are based on similar considerations.

Other units can be considered as fixed-job organizations; that is, units with a specific function to perform (e.g., orientation, registration, financial aids). Effectiveness is determined by the number of specific tasks accomplished. Learning skills centers or special transportation services for the mobility impaired meet this definition. Community examples include fire protection, emergency ambulance services, and snow removal. In these organizations, effectiveness judgments are based on how many students were tested or transported, and how many fires, ambulance calls, and snow storms required responses.

The Anthony and Hertlingzer (1980) framework can be used to identify and design financial management strategies. On any given campus, units designated as business-like, fixed-resource, or fixed-job will vary. Each student affairs division must identify the units, services, or programs that correspond to the Anthony and Hertlingzer categories. Institutions that rely extensively on the fee-for-service models and user charges may have more units in the business-like category than institutions that fund programs and services from general fund allocations.

MONITORING FINANCIAL MANAGEMENT IN STUDENT AFFAIRS

Although ambiguity tends to characterize many aspects of life in IHEs (Cohen & March, 1974), financial management is one of the few processes that must meet the expectations for tightly coupled, bureaucratic performance in order to be judged effective (Kuh, 1983). Therefore, no matter which NFP definition is adopted, fiscal responsibility requires that someone continually monitor the use of resources (McClenny & Chaffee, 1985). Monitoring serves at least two purposes. First, if unusual, unanticipated pressures are placed on resources in one area, the chief student affairs officer or the CSAO's representative will be informed about relative expenditure levels throughout the organization and can authorize—after consultation with the chief financial affairs officer—a transfer of funds to meet the fiscal shortfall. Second, although it is expected that every account manager will be fiscally responsible, this will not always be the case.

To be an effective budget control mechanism, monitoring should be performed at three levels: (a) account manager; (b) student affairs division (CSAO); and (c) institution. In effective organizations, responsibility and authority are found at the point closest to the action—the program or activity level (Peters & Waterman, 1982). Through periodic review (e.g., monthly) of a "report against the budget form" that reflects expenditures, a manager can review encumbered funds, projected expenses, and budget remainder to determine whether the unit is expending resources, such as salaries or wages, at a rate compatible with unit objectives and within the limits of the annual allocation (Powell,

1980). In this sense, monthly reports are a "spending barometer" (Blair, 1981).

Ultimately, the CSAO is responsible for making certain that the division of student affairs conforms to the "every tub on its own bottom" principle of fiscal management (N. Pusey in Kaludis, 1973). That is, no unit can spend more than has been allocated without authorization. An overrun in a student affairs budget line will be an embarrassment for the account manager and possibly difficult for the institution to absorb. Careful periodic monitoring at the division level can often identify likely budget overruns early enough so that corrective action can be taken.

The third level of budget review, institution or campus-level monitoring, occurs less frequently than that performed by an account manager. Two reviews are common: (a) a mid-year examination prompted by the need to meet exigencies perhaps created by revenue shortfalls or overexpenditures in other units, and (b) the annual budget review cycle during which time the next year's budget is planned and prepared.

Budget Monitoring Strategies

Evaluation of fiscal responsibility is almost always performed at some level near the end of a budget cycle (or at some other institutionalized time). However, informal, irregular, infrequent, anecdotal observations occur on an ongoing basis and influence the distribution of resources within the division of student affairs. These reviews may be conducted by the CSAO or by the division's designated fiscal officer. On occasion, reviews of the student affairs budget may be conducted by others on campus. Reviews may be more or less formal (e.g., a formal hearing or informal conversation over coffee). The degree of formality of the review is an institutional culture issue (Kuh & Whitt, 1988).

Ideally, student affairs managers should be engaged in two kinds of monitoring: (a) quantitative and (b) qualitative. In a quantitative review, the manager focuses on variances in the amount of activity taking place and notes variations in expected revenues. For example, fall semester income from individually sold meals by the food service may drop behind projected revenues and necessitate a price increase on some items in the spring semester or some cost cutting measures to maintain an acceptable revenues-expense balance.

Quantitative data in the form of efficiency indices tend to be more difficult to obtain in most areas of student affairs although in some units—such as financial aids, registration, and the food service—efficiency measures could be useful for monitoring purposes. For example, comparative information about the costs of computerized student registration and on-site, mass registration could help determine if a proposed change would result in processing of more student registration records in fewer hours, thus increasing the cost-effectiveness of the process.

Financial monitoring should also include a qualitative dimension. That is, although actual and predicted rates of resource expenditures are important indices, other assessments—particularly those that may more directly reflect the quality of student life—should also inform the monitoring process. This information may be intuitive or acquired after observations and exposure to streams of anecdotal information. Seasoned student affairs staff may have hunches about whether certain processes and procedures constitute an effective use of resources. Although advance computerized registration may prove efficient on some criteria (batch processing speed, reallocation of instructional resources to oversubscribed courses), other equally desirable conditions may be threatened. For example, computerized registration typically is related to an unusually high proportion of students (perhaps as much as 40%) who must revise schedules after the start of classes to accommodate changes in career plans or intervening events (personal cash flow problems necessitating fewer credit hours, courses taken during the preceding summer necessitating selection of different courses, etc.). Replacing the mass registration event—a time when faculty, students, and staff have an opportunity to see and visit with one another—with an almost anonymous activity that reduces contact between students and faculty may not be worth the cost difference realized by computerizing the process.

Ideally, account monitoring is a continuous activity that effectively ignores symbolic and "real" academic year demarcations. For all practical purposes, one fiscal year or budget cycle spills over into the next as far as setting priorities and making plans are concerned. That is, although the "every tub on its own bottom" principle must be observed, short-range unit planning (program development, staff resignation or retirement, recruitment cycles, and equipment and capital maintenance requirements) cannot proceed without joining consideration of the current budget cycle with the next cycle and perhaps beyond.

In summary, periodic monitoring at various levels can suggest necessary action by managers such as reallocation of resources from an overfunded area to an oversubscribed program to respond to possible budget overruns. Monitoring can alert campus budget officers to potential opportunities to reallocate resources, such as a projected year-end surplus, or to problems such as cost overruns or deficits in auxiliary functions, such as the bookstore, due to higher midsemester attrition rates.

APPROACHES FOR TRACKING THE EFFICACY OF FINANCIAL MANAGEMENT IN STUDENT AFFAIRS

Any "model" or strategy for evaluation of financial management must be sensitive to context-specific factors (Borchert & Mickelson, 1973). Has the student affairs division been traditionally under- or overfunded? What revenue pressures are currently influencing, or are likely to influence, resource use patterns? Does the campus culture value the contributions of student affairs? Do faculty perceive that student affairs is in competition with academic programs for resources?

Four approaches can be used to examine the quality of financial management practices and can be modified to accommodate particular contextual factors. The first is some form of campus-level review in which a task force—made up of faculty, students, and administrators—is charged with reviewing how resources are used by the student affairs division. Stand-alone reviews are unusual (see Moxley & Duke, 1986, for a student affairs example). Most often, campus-level reviews are incorporated in the annual budgeting cycle. It is easy for student affairs staff to view these annual rituals as nothing more than a "show and tell" exercise, but CSAOs are encouraged to use these and other opportunities to tie resources to indices of the quality of student life.

The second approach takes the form of division-initiated site visits in which highly regarded student affairs leaders serve as consultants. They are assumed to have the expertise to evaluate comparative resource allocation patterns. Their judgments are necessarily delimited by context-specific factors, and are only as credible as those rendering the judgments. Site visitors should be selected for their professional expertise and accomplishments, not because they are close personal friends of the CSAO.

Routine external accreditation visits provide another opportunity for student affairs units to obtain feedback about resource use. If accreditation is to be more than a perfunctory exercise, however, CSAOs should exert their prerogative and make sure that someone with student affairs experience is included on the accreditation team.

The last commonly used estimate of student affairs resources are consumer surveys, in which students and other users of student affairs services are invited to comment on the quality and accessibility of services. Survey data are best used as an adjunct to other processes that allow more in-depth analysis of actual expenditures rather than perceptual information typically assembled from responses to surveys.

Financial Management Checklist

The following questions provide a starting point for those who wish to evaluate financial management practices in their division of student affairs. This list is not exhaustive, and the questions will be more or less relevant depending on an institution's history and culture (Kuh & Whitt, 1988) and the current circumstances the student affairs division faces. The questions may be more revealing when used in concert with the standards for student affairs developed by the Council for the Advancement of Standards for Student Services/Development Programs (1986).

A. *What does the student affairs budget support at present?* Before an analysis of the management of student affairs resources can be initiated, those involved in the process must have an overview of all the activities the student affairs division addresses. Even a superficial understanding of the whole will allow some insight into how the various units and programs complement each other and justify their support.

B. *Does the student affairs budget reflect institutional values and priorities?* Resources are best invested in programs and services that are directly linked to the institution's mission and educational purposes. Defending the student affairs budget at the campus level will be easier if it can be demonstrated that student affairs programs and students' out-of-class experiences promote attainment of the institution's educational purposes (Balderston, 1974; Dressel, 1973; Kuh et al., 1989).

C. *Are resource allocations and patterns of resource use throughout the division consistent with institutional priorities?* In institutions with a broad liberal arts mission, most faculty members are likely to view student development programming as being consistent with the institution's mission (Kuh, Shedd, & Whitt, 1987). Do resource use patterns demonstrate that targeted groups of students are receiving the intended resources? For example, are funds earmarked and expended for minority programming and retention efforts?

D. *Are patterns of resource use efficient?* Efficient resource use is difficult to determine. When available, unit or institutional comparisons may generate useful data. A historical review of budget allocations, innovations, or new programs along with expenditure patterns can also be instructive. The reputation of the unit administrator plays a significant role in judgments about efficient resource management. For example, an admissions office that has internally reallocated resources to support alternative recruitment strategies in response to market changes is usually considered efficient and responsive. However, units that always request new resources to respond to changing conditions invite criticism about the unit administrator's financial management ability.

E. *Do patterns of resource use vary according to the nature of the activity?* Student affairs programs and services tend to be elastic; that is, accommodating additional students in some areas such as leadership training or intramurals does not usually require additional funds. However, some functions (financial aids, residence halls, security) will require additional resources to accommodate additional students.

F. *Are some costs avoidable?* Many services or programs continue despite changing campus circumstances or enrollment patterns. Over the past few years the number of veterans enrolling on most residential campuses has declined. Can some staffing or program costs be avoided through reorganization or program consolidation? Should multiple copies of midterm grades be ordered for distribution and files prior to the development of a computer record system? Additional printing may be unnecessary if academic advisors have computer access to the information.

G. *Can some programs be discontinued?* Most student affairs units have responded to the needs of increasingly heterogeneous groups of students by adding specialized programs and services. Too often, these programs are merely added to an already full plate of activities for student affairs staff. Terminating one or more programs may free resources that are better used to support other activities. At the least, staff will have more time to emphasize program quality (Kuh, 1985).

H. *What are the foregone opportunities for students, staff, and faculty if a program or service is modified or terminated? Can these be portrayed in understandable cost-benefit ratios?* Before a program or service is terminated, the likely effects of the absence of the program or service should be estimated. Little is gained if an institutionalized service is no longer available but students or faculty continue to request the service. For example, to conserve resources the registrar may wish to discontinue issuing faculty and student identification cards. But if students and faculty are required to show identification to use the library, to eat in the cafeteria, or to use the health center, continuing the ID card service may be necessary. Reallocation of resources (supplies and expense money, part of a staff member's time) may not be worth the effort if debilitating public relations problems are associated with program termination.

I. *What opportunities can be enhanced, and for whom, by providing additional services or programs?* If additional resources are obtained either through internal reallocation or a base budget addition, what will be the likely benefits for students or other consumers of the program or service? Some unforeseen opportunities may be overlooked, such as the contribution a campus day-care center may make to student retention goals.

J. *Can some services or programs pay their own way? Are alternative funding sources being pursued vigorously?* Because funding levels are not likely to increase beyond modest cost-of-living rates, pressure will grow for units to cut costs or increase revenues. Legal and health services may be targets of opportunity on some campuses. The costs of these services have escalated, and many colleges have been able to endure the transition between campus-subsidized services to user fees or consumer purchased services—pay as you go. Student affairs professionals must become more aggressive in soliciting funds from external sources through appeals to alumni and friends and through grant proposals.

K. *Do conditions exist that point to a shift in demand for student affairs resources that would influence the share of institutional support for student affairs?* Demographic projections (Hodgkinson, 1985) suggest that if institutions are to maintain steady enrollments, more first-generation and minority students must enroll in college. To respond sensitively to an increasingly pluralistic student body, additional resources for learning skills programs may be required.

L. *Who is responsible for monitoring and evaluating the different aspects of student affairs fiscal and human resources?* Someone in the student affairs division must be formally charged with periodic monitoring of resource use. In many instances, this will be the CSAO. On some large campuses, a staff member from the CSAO's office could perform this responsibility.

M. *What "model" or strategies are most appropriate, given the local context, for accountability, performance monitoring, and evaluation?* Over time, routine practices become institutionalized. No single model or approach can be effective in every environment. In some institutions, the annual budget review cycle is the most appropriate occasion for formally estimating efficiency and effectiveness. Realistically, most student affairs units do not invest considerable time in estimating the quality of financial management simply because there are too many other, more important things to do. The best rule is to spend at least as much time as academic units do in assembling data for the president's cabinet and trustee consumption.

N. *Do financial limitations inhibit the division from making even greater contributions to the institution's mission and the quality of campus life?* Although it is unrealistic to expect that student affairs (or any campus unit for that matter) is likely to receive substantial base budget increases in the next decade, the financial manager must be cognizant of what the student affairs unit is unable to do because of thinly stretched resources. In the event that resources can be reallocated from within, a compelling rationale is needed to justify targeting resources for one unit and not others that also have a legitimate claim for additional support.

CONCLUSION

The student affairs manager must identify and take advantage of opportunities to demonstrate how the resources allocated to student affairs contribute to the quality of student life and the attainment of institutional goals. Skillful, financially astute student affairs staff recognize the value of quantitative and qualitative indices and the need to obtain relevant data from multiple sources. The greatest challenge is to use the base budget as wisely as possible and direct limited resources to those programs and services that serve directly the institution's purposes.

Student affairs organizations well positioned to respond to financial challenges share five characteristics: (a) a clear understanding of the operative institutional mission and goals (Conrad, 1974); (b) the ability to articulate persuasively how student affairs programs and services contribute to the attainment of the institution's educational purposes; (c) an understanding of the not-for-profit organizational model and its applicability to student affairs; (d) effective financial management control procedures at several levels; and (e) a mind set that interprets the constantly changing higher education environment as challenging and inspiring, not threatening.

REFERENCES

Anthony, R.N., & Hertlingzer, R.E. (1980). *Management control in nonprofit organizations.* Homewood, IL: Irwin.

Anthony, R.N., & Young, D.W. (1984). *Management and control in nonprofit organizations.* Homewood, IL: Irwin.

Balderston, F.E. (1974). *Managing today's university.* San Francisco: Jossey-Bass.

Blair, J.P. (1981). Spending rates as evaluative tools. *Evaluation Review, 5,* 712–719.

Borchert, F.R., & Mickelson, U.C. (1973). Creating a financial management system. In G. Kaludis, (Ed.), *Strategies for budgeting.* New Directions for Higher Education, No. 2. San Francisco: Jossey-Bass.

Carnegie Council on Policy Studies in Higher Education. (1980). *Three thousand futures: The next twenty years for higher education.* San Francisco: Jossey-Bass.

Caruthers, J.K., & Orwig, M. (1979). *Budgeting in higher education.* AAHE-ERIC Higher Education Research Report No. 3. Washington, DC: American Association of Higher Education.

Cohen, M.D., & March, J.G. (1974). *Leadership and ambiguity: The American college president.* New York: McGraw-Hill.

Conrad, C.F. (1974). University goals: An operative report. *Journal of Higher Education, 35,* 504–516.

Conrad, C.F., & Wilson, R.F. (1985). *Academic program review: Institutional approaches, expectations, and controversies.* ASHE-ERIC Higher Education Report, No. 5. Washington, DC: Association for the Study of Higher Education.

Council for the Advancement of Standards for Student Services/Development Programs. (1986). *CAS standards and guidelines for student services/development programs.* Iowa City: American College Testing Program.

Douglas, D.O. (1983). Fiscal resource management: Background and relevance for student affairs. In T.K. Miller, R.B. Winston, & W.R. Mendenhall (Eds.), *Administration and leadership in higher education* (pp. 375–397). Muncie, IN: Accelerated Development.

Dressel, P.L. (1973). Measuring the benefits of student personnel work. *Journal of Higher Education, 44,* 15–26.

Forbes, R.H. (1974). Cost effectiveness analysis: Primer and guidelines. *Evaluation Review, 10,* 29–44.

Frances, C. (1985). Major trends shaping the outlook for higher education. *AAHE Bulletin, 38*(4), 3–7.

Georgiou, P. (1973). The goal paradigm and notes toward a counter paradigm. *Administrative Science Quarterly, 18,* 291–310.

Hammond, M.F., & Thompkins, L.D. (1986). The dilemma of the state university in the 1980's. *College Board Review, 139,* 12–19, 32–33.

Harpel, R.L. (1978). Evaluating from a management perspective. In G.R. Hanson (Ed.), *Evaluating program effectiveness* (pp. 19–33). New Directions for Student Services, No. 1. San Francisco: Jossey-Bass.

Hodgkinson, H.L. (1985). *All one system: Demographics of education, kindergarten through graduate school.* Washington, DC: Institute for Educational Leadership.

Hossler, D. (1984). *Enrollment management.* New York: College Board.

Kaludis, G. (1973). Emerging principles for budgeting. In G. Kaludis (Ed.), *Strategies for budgeting* (pp. 97–102). New Directions for Higher Education, No. 2. San Francisco: Jossey-Bass.

Kauffman, J.F. (1984). Assessing the quality of student services. In R.A. Scott (Ed.), *Determining the effectiveness of campus services* (pp. 23–36). New Directions for Institutional Research, No. 41. San Francisco: Jossey-Bass.

King, B.G. (1975). Cost effective analysis: Implications for accountants. In R.T. Golembiewski & J. Rubin (Eds.), *Public budgeting and finance: Readings in theory and practice* (pp. 396–406). Itasca, IL: Peacock.

Kuh, G.D. (1983). Guiding assumptions about student affairs organizations. In G. Kuh (Ed.), *Understanding student affairs organizations* (pp. 15–26). New Directions for Student Services, No. 23. San Francisco: Jossey-Bass.

Kuh, G.D. (1985). What is extraordinary about ordinary student affairs organizations. *NASPA Journal, 23*(2), 31–45.

Kuh, G.D., Schuh, J.H., Andreas, R., Blake, J.H., Lyons, J.W., Strange, C.C., Whitt, E.J., Krehbiel, L., & MacKay, K.A. (1989, March). *Institutional factors and conditions associated with high quality out-of-class experiences of undergraduate students.* Paper presented at the annual meeting of the National Association of Student Personnel Administrators, Denver.

Kuh, G.D., Shedd, J.D., & Whitt, E.J. (1987). Student affairs and liberal education: Unrecognized common law partners. *Journal of College Student Personnel, 28,* 252–260.

Kuh, G.D., & Whitt, E.J. (1988). *The invisible tapestry: Culture in American colleges and universities.* ASHE-ERIC Higher Education Report No. 1. Washington, DC: Association for the Study of Higher Education.

McClenny, B.N., & Chaffee, E.E. (1985). Integrating academic planning and budgeting. In D.F. Campbell (Ed.), *Strengthening financial management* (pp. 7–20). New Directions for Community Colleges, No. 50. San Francisco: Jossey-Bass.

Meisinger, R.J., & Dubeck, L.W. (1984). *College and university budgeting: An introduction for faculty and academic administrators.* Washington, DC: National Association of College and University Business Officers.

Moxley, L.S., & Duke, B.W. (1986). Setting priorities for student affairs programs for budgetary purposes: A case study. *NASPA Journal, 23*(4), 21–28.

Pembroke, W.J. (1985). Fiscal constraints on program development. In M.J. Barr, L.A. Keating, & Associates (Eds.), *Developing effective student service programs* (pp. 83–107). San Francisco: Jossey-Bass.

Peters, T.J., & Waterman, R.H. (1982). *In search of excellence: Lessons from America's best run companies.* New York: Harper & Row.

Peterson, R.D. (1986). The anatomy of cost-effectiveness analysis. *Evaluation Review, 10,* 29–44.

Pfeffer, J., & Salancik, G.R. (1974). Organizational decision making as a political process: The case of the university budget. *Administrative Science Quarterly, 19,* 135 151.

Powell, R.M. (1980). *Budgetary control procedures for institutions.* Notre Dame, IN: University of Notre Dame Press.

Scott, R.A. (1978). *Lords, squires, and yeomen: Collegiate middle managers and their organizations.* AAHE-ERIC/Higher Education Research Report No. 7. Washington, DC: American Association for Higher Education.

Thompson, M.S., & Fortess, E.E. (1980). Cost effectiveness analysis in health program evaluation. *Evaluation Review, 4,* 549–568.

Tonn, J.C. (1978). Political behavior in higher education budgeting. *Journal of Higher Education, 49,* 575–587.

Vinter, R.D., & Kish, R.K. (1984). *Budgeting for not for profit organizations.* New York: Free Press.

Wildavsky, A. (1974). *The politics of budgetary process.* Boston: Little, Brown.